This journal is dedicated to those of you who are carrying more than you let anyone see.
May this journal give you space to exhale, reflect, and return to yourself.

I see you. I appreciate you. Now it's time to see and appreciate yourself.

Hey there,

Every time I sit with someone who feels overwhelmed, exhausted, or stretched thin, there's a moment where I can almost see the weight on their shoulders. Despite saying "I'm fine." It shows up in how they talk about their day, sometimes it shows up in the rise of their shoulders. And sometimes it's the long pause or sigh before they say anything else.

Most of time I will tell them "just take a moment and breathe"

This journal is that moment in physical form.
It's not meant to fix you in 90-days. It's here to help you notice yourself again, all of you. Your feelings, your needs, your energy, your truth. Stress resiliency is ultimately about learning to navigate your inner world with more compassion, awareness, and groundedness.

Over these next few months, you'll move through small but powerful reflection practices that not only help you track patterns but reconnect you to what matters, and slowly rebuild the relationship you have with yourself while breaking up with the relationship you have with stress.

You don't have to do it perfectly. You don't have to fill every page. You just have to show up honestly.

Take your time. Move gently. Let this be the space where you exhale.
I'm grateful you're here.

Candice

JAN FEB MAR APR MAY JUN JUL AUG SEP OCT NOV DEC
1 2 3 4 5 6 7 8 9 10 11 12 13 14 15 16 17 18 19 20 21 22 23 24 25 26 27 28 29 30 31

Daily Morning Reset

(For mental clarity + emotional grounding)

Today, my body feels…

☐ Tense
☐ Rested
☐ Scattered
☐ Heavy
☐ Neutral
☐ Something else: _____

One thing weighing on me today is…

_____
_____
_____
_____
_____

Emotion I'm carrying into today:

_____
_____
_____
_____
_____

What I need emotionally right now:

☐ Space
☐ Encouragement
☐ Boundaries
☐ Rest
☐ Focus
☐ Connection
☐ Other: _____

My intention for today:
A sentence or two that feels doable, gentle, and honest.

_____
_____
_____

A micro-practice to begin the day:
(Choose one)

- 1-minute grounding breath

- Soften your jaw + drop your shoulders

- Step outside for 3 deep breaths

- Name three things supporting you today

Daily Evening Reflection Pages
(For emotional processing + nervous system unwinding)

Where did stress show up today?

Body: _____
Mind: _____
Emotions: _____

How did I respond?

☐ Reacted quickly
☐ Shut down
☐ Over-functioned
☐ Avoided
☐ Paused
☐ Responded intentionally

Notes:
_____
_____
_____

What part of me needed more care?

_____
_____
_____

A moment I'm proud of today:
_____
_____
_____
_____
_____
_____

Something I want to release tonight:
_____
_____
_____
_____
_____
_____

Notes:
_____
_____
_____

Closing breath cue:
Inhale for 4, hold for 2, exhale for 6 — repeat 3 times.

JAN	FEB	MAR	APR	MAY	JUN	JUL	AUG	SEP	OCT	NOV	DEC

1 2 3 4 5 6 7 8 9 10 11 12 13 14 15 16 17 18 19 20 21 22 23 24 25 26 27 28 29 30 31

Daily Morning Reset

(For mental clarity + emotional grounding)

Today, my body feels…

☐ Tense
☐ Rested
☐ Scattered
☐ Heavy
☐ Neutral
☐ Something else: _____

One thing weighing on me today is…

_____
_____
_____
_____

Emotion I'm carrying into today:

_____
_____
_____
_____

What I need emotionally right now:

☐ Space
☐ Encouragement
☐ Boundaries
☐ Rest
☐ Focus
☐ Connection
☐ Other: _____

My intention for today:
A sentence or two that feels doable, gentle, and honest.

_____
_____
_____

A micro-practice to begin the day:
(Choose one)

- 1-minute grounding breath

- Soften your jaw + drop your shoulders

- Step outside for 3 deep breaths

- Name three things supporting you today

Daily Evening Reflection Pages
(For emotional processing + nervous system unwinding)

Where did stress show up today?

Body: _____
Mind: _____
Emotions: _____

How did I respond?

- ☐ Reacted quickly
- ☐ Shut down
- ☐ Over-functioned
- ☐ Avoided
- ☐ Paused
- ☐ Responded intentionally

Notes:
_____
_____
_____

What part of me needed more care?

_____
_____
_____
_____

A moment I'm proud of today:
_____
_____
_____
_____
_____

Something I want to release tonight:
_____
_____
_____
_____
_____

Notes:
_____
_____
_____

Closing breath cue:
Inhale for 4, hold for 2, exhale for 6 — repeat 3 times.

| JAN | FEB | MAR | APR | MAY | JUN | JUL | AUG | SEP | OCT | NOV | DEC |

1 2 3 4 5 6 7 8 9 10 11 12 13 14 15 16 17 18 19 20 21 22 23 24 25 26 27 28 29 30 31

Daily Morning Reset
(For mental clarity + emotional grounding)

Today, my body feels…

☐ Tense
☐ Rested
☐ Scattered
☐ Heavy
☐ Neutral
☐ Something else: _____

One thing weighing on me today is…

_____
_____
_____
_____
_____

Emotion I'm carrying into today:

_____
_____
_____
_____
_____

What I need emotionally right now:
- ☐ Space
- ☐ Encouragement
- ☐ Boundaries
- ☐ Rest
- ☐ Focus
- ☐ Connection
- ☐ Other: _____

My intention for today:
A sentence or two that feels doable, gentle, and honest.

_____
_____
_____

A micro-practice to begin the day:
(Choose one)

- 1-minute grounding breath

- Soften your jaw + drop your shoulders

- Step outside for 3 deep breaths

- Name three things supporting you today

Daily Evening Reflection Pages
(For emotional processing + nervous system unwinding)

Where did stress show up today?

Body: _____
Mind: _____
Emotions: _____

How did I respond?

☐ Reacted quickly
☐ Shut down
☐ Over-functioned
☐ Avoided
☐ Paused
☐ Responded intentionally

Notes:
_____
_____
_____

What part of me needed more care?
_____
_____
_____
_____

A moment I'm proud of today:
_____
_____
_____
_____
_____

Something I want to release tonight:
_____
_____
_____
_____
_____

Notes:
_____
_____
_____

Closing breath cue:

Inhale for 4, hold for 2, exhale for 6 — repeat 3 times.

JAN　FEB　MAR　APR　MAY　JUN　JUL　AUG　SEP　OCT　NOV　DEC
1　2　3　4　5　6　7　8　9　10　11　12　13　14　15　16　17　18　19　20　21　22　23　24　25　26　27　28　29　30　31

Daily Morning Reset
(For mental clarity + emotional grounding)

Today, my body feels…

☐ Tense
☐ Rested
☐ Scattered
☐ Heavy
☐ Neutral
☐ Something else: _____

One thing weighing on me today is…

_____
_____
_____
_____
_____

Emotion I'm carrying into today:

_____
_____
_____
_____

What I need emotionally right now:

☐ Space
☐ Encouragement
☐ Boundaries
☐ Rest
☐ Focus
☐ Connection
☐ Other: _____

My intention for today:
A sentence or two that feels doable, gentle, and honest.

_____
_____
_____

A micro-practice to begin the day:
(Choose one)

- 1-minute grounding breath

- Soften your jaw + drop your shoulders

- Step outside for 3 deep breaths

- Name three things supporting you today

Daily Evening Reflection Pages
(For emotional processing + nervous system unwinding)

Where did stress show up today?

Body: _____
Mind: _____
Emotions: _____

How did I respond?

☐ Reacted quickly
☐ Shut down
☐ Over-functioned
☐ Avoided
☐ Paused
☐ Responded intentionally

Notes:
_____
_____
_____

What part of me needed more care?
_____
_____
_____
_____

A moment I'm proud of today:
_____
_____
_____
_____
_____

Something I want to release tonight:
_____
_____
_____
_____
_____

Notes:
_____
_____

Closing breath cue:

Inhale for 4, hold for 2, exhale for 6 — repeat 3 times.

JAN	FEB	MAR	APR	MAY	JUN	JUL	AUG	SEP	OCT	NOV	DEC

1 2 3 4 5 6 7 8 9 10 11 12 13 14 15 16 17 18 19 20 21 22 23 24 25 26 27 28 29 30 31

Daily Morning Reset

(For mental clarity + emotional grounding)

Today, my body feels…

☐ Tense
☐ Rested
☐ Scattered
☐ Heavy
☐ Neutral
☐ Something else: _____

One thing weighing on me today is…

_____
_____
_____
_____
_____

Emotion I'm carrying into today:

_____
_____
_____
_____

What I need emotionally right now:

☐ Space
☐ Encouragement
☐ Boundaries
☐ Rest
☐ Focus
☐ Connection
☐ Other: _____

My intention for today:
A sentence or two that feels doable, gentle, and honest.

_____
_____
_____

A micro-practice to begin the day:
(Choose one)

- 1-minute grounding breath

- Soften your jaw + drop your shoulders

- Step outside for 3 deep breaths

- Name three things supporting you today

Daily Evening Reflection Pages
(For emotional processing + nervous system unwinding)

Where did stress show up today?

Body: _____
Mind: _____
Emotions: _____

How did I respond?

☐ Reacted quickly
☐ Shut down
☐ Over-functioned
☐ Avoided
☐ Paused
☐ Responded intentionally

Notes:
_____
_____
_____

What part of me needed more care?

_____
_____
_____

A moment I'm proud of today:
_____
_____
_____
_____
_____

Something I want to release tonight:
_____
_____
_____
_____
_____

Notes:
_____
_____

Closing breath cue:
Inhale for 4, hold for 2, exhale for 6 — repeat 3 times.

| JAN | FEB | MAR | APR | MAY | JUN | JUL | AUG | SEP | OCT | NOV | DEC |

1 2 3 4 5 6 7 8 9 10 11 12 13 14 15 16 17 18 19 20 21 22 23 24 25 26 27 28 29 30 31

Daily Morning Reset
(For mental clarity + emotional grounding)

Today, my body feels...

☐ Tense
☐ Rested
☐ Scattered
☐ Heavy
☐ Neutral
☐ Something else: _____

One thing weighing on me today is...

_____
_____
_____
_____
_____

Emotion I'm carrying into today:

_____
_____
_____
_____
_____

What I need emotionally right now:

☐ Space
☐ Encouragement
☐ Boundaries
☐ Rest
☐ Focus
☐ Connection
☐ Other: _____

My intention for today:
A sentence or two that feels doable, gentle, and honest.

_____
_____
_____

A micro-practice to begin the day:
(Choose one)

- 1-minute grounding breath

- Soften your jaw + drop your shoulders

- Step outside for 3 deep breaths

- Name three things supporting you today

Daily Evening Reflection Pages
(For emotional processing + nervous system unwinding)

Where did stress show up today?

Body: _____
Mind: _____
Emotions: _____

How did I respond?

- ☐ Reacted quickly
- ☐ Shut down
- ☐ Over-functioned
- ☐ Avoided
- ☐ Paused
- ☐ Responded intentionally

Notes:
_____
_____
_____

What part of me needed more care?
_____
_____
_____

A moment I'm proud of today:
_____
_____
_____
_____
_____
_____

Something I want to release tonight:
_____
_____
_____
_____
_____
_____

Notes:
_____
_____
_____

Closing breath cue:

Inhale for 4, hold for 2, exhale for 6 — repeat 3 times.

JAN	FEB	MAR	APR	MAY	JUN	JUL	AUG	SEP	OCT	NOV	DEC

1 2 3 4 5 6 7 8 9 10 11 12 13 14 15 16 17 18 19 20 21 22 23 24 25 26 27 28 29 30 31

Daily Morning Reset

(For mental clarity + emotional grounding)

Today, my body feels…

- ☐ Tense
- ☐ Rested
- ☐ Scattered
- ☐ Heavy
- ☐ Neutral
- ☐ Something else: _____

One thing weighing on me today is…

_____
_____
_____
_____
_____

Emotion I'm carrying into today:

_____
_____
_____
_____
_____

What I need emotionally right now:

☐ Space
☐ Encouragement
☐ Boundaries
☐ Rest
☐ Focus
☐ Connection
☐ Other: _____

My intention for today:

A sentence or two that feels doable, gentle, and honest.

_____
_____
_____

A micro-practice to begin the day:

(Choose one)

- 1-minute grounding breath

- Soften your jaw + drop your shoulders

- Step outside for 3 deep breaths

- Name three things supporting you today

Daily Evening Reflection Pages
(For emotional processing + nervous system unwinding)

Where did stress show up today?

Body: _____
Mind: _____
Emotions: _____

How did I respond?

☐ Reacted quickly
☐ Shut down
☐ Over-functioned
☐ Avoided
☐ Paused
☐ Responded intentionally

Notes:
_____
_____
_____

What part of me needed more care?

_____
_____
_____
_____

A moment I'm proud of today:

_____
_____
_____
_____
_____

Something I want to release tonight:

_____
_____
_____
_____
_____

Notes:

_____
_____
_____

Closing breath cue:

Inhale for 4, hold for 2, exhale for 6 — repeat 3 times.

Weekly Reflection

Energy Check-In

What drained me this week?

_____
_____
_____

What restored me this week?

_____
_____
_____

Emotional Patterns I Noticed

- When did I override myself?

- When did I honor my capacity?

- What emotion repeated most?

Notes:
_____
_____

A boundary I need for next week:
_____
_____

One small shift that would support me next week:
_____
_____

Weekly Stress Pattern Awareness Worksheet

What My Stress Cycle This Week Looked Like:

Trigger → Reaction → Emotion → Behavior → Aftermath

Trigger: _____
Reaction: _____
Emotion: _____
Behavior: _____
Aftermath: _____

Trigger: _____
Reaction: _____
Emotion: _____
Behavior: _____
Aftermath: _____

Trigger: _____
Reaction: _____
Emotion: _____
Behavior: _____
Aftermath: _____

What my body did under stress:

☐ Tight chest
☐ Stomach tension
☐ Shallow breathing
☐ Head pressure
☐ Frozen / shut down
☐ Other: _____

What I needed in those moments:

☐ Slowness
☐ Clarity
☐ Space
☐ Reassurance
☐ Regulation
☐ Boundaries

Notes:

_____
_____

JAN FEB MAR APR MAY JUN JUL AUG SEP OCT NOV DEC
1 2 3 4 5 6 7 8 9 10 11 12 13 14 15 16 17 18 19 20 21 22 23 24 25 26 27 28 29 30 31

Daily Morning Reset

(For mental clarity + emotional grounding)

Today, my body feels…

☐ Tense
☐ Rested
☐ Scattered
☐ Heavy
☐ Neutral
☐ Something else: _____

One thing weighing on me today is…

_____
_____
_____
_____
_____

Emotion I'm carrying into today:

_____
_____
_____
_____
_____

What I need emotionally right now:

☐ Space
☐ Encouragement
☐ Boundaries
☐ Rest
☐ Focus
☐ Connection
☐ Other: _____

My intention for today:
A sentence or two that feels doable, gentle, and honest.

_____
_____
_____

A micro-practice to begin the day:
(Choose one)

- 1-minute grounding breath

- Soften your jaw + drop your shoulders

- Step outside for 3 deep breaths

- Name three things supporting you today

Daily Evening Reflection Pages
(For emotional processing + nervous system unwinding)

Where did stress show up today?

Body: _____
Mind: _____
Emotions: _____

How did I respond?

☐ Reacted quickly
☐ Shut down
☐ Over-functioned
☐ Avoided
☐ Paused
☐ Responded intentionally

Notes:
_____
_____
_____

What part of me needed more care?
_____
_____
_____
_____

A moment I'm proud of today:
_____
_____
_____
_____
_____

Something I want to release tonight:
_____
_____
_____
_____
_____

Notes:
_____
_____
_____

Closing breath cue:

Inhale for 4, hold for 2, exhale for 6 — repeat 3 times.

JAN	FEB	MAR	APR	MAY	JUN	JUL	AUG	SEP	OCT	NOV	DEC

1 2 3 4 5 6 7 8 9 10 11 12 13 14 15 16 17 18 19 20 21 22 23 24 25 26 27 28 29 30 31

Daily Morning Reset
(For mental clarity + emotional grounding)

Today, my body feels…

☐ Tense
☐ Rested
☐ Scattered
☐ Heavy
☐ Neutral
☐ Something else: _____

One thing weighing on me today is…

_____
_____
_____
_____
_____

Emotion I'm carrying into today:

_____
_____
_____
_____
_____

What I need emotionally right now:

☐ Space
☐ Encouragement
☐ Boundaries
☐ Rest
☐ Focus
☐ Connection
☐ Other: _____

My intention for today:
A sentence or two that feels doable, gentle, and honest.

_____
_____
_____

A micro-practice to begin the day:
(Choose one)

- 1-minute grounding breath

- Soften your jaw + drop your shoulders

- Step outside for 3 deep breaths

- Name three things supporting you today

Daily Evening Reflection Pages
(For emotional processing + nervous system unwinding)

Where did stress show up today?

Body: _____
Mind: _____
Emotions: _____

How did I respond?

☐ Reacted quickly
☐ Shut down
☐ Over-functioned
☐ Avoided
☐ Paused
☐ Responded intentionally

Notes:
_____
_____
_____

What part of me needed more care?

_____
_____
_____
_____

A moment I'm proud of today:
_____
_____
_____
_____
_____

Something I want to release tonight:
_____
_____
_____
_____
_____

Notes:
_____
_____
_____

Closing breath cue:

Inhale for 4, hold for 2, exhale for 6 — repeat 3 times.

JAN	FEB	MAR	APR	MAY	JUN	JUL	AUG	SEP	OCT	NOV	DEC

1 2 3 4 5 6 7 8 9 10 11 12 13 14 15 16 17 18 19 20 21 22 23 24 25 26 27 28 29 30 31

Daily Morning Reset
(For mental clarity + emotional grounding)

Today, my body feels…

☐ Tense
☐ Rested
☐ Scattered
☐ Heavy
☐ Neutral
☐ Something else: _____

One thing weighing on me today is…

_____
_____
_____
_____
_____

Emotion I'm carrying into today:

_____
_____
_____
_____

What I need emotionally right now:

☐ Space
☐ Encouragement
☐ Boundaries
☐ Rest
☐ Focus
☐ Connection
☐ Other: _____

My intention for today:
A sentence or two that feels doable, gentle, and honest.

_____
_____
_____

A micro-practice to begin the day:
(Choose one)

- 1-minute grounding breath

- Soften your jaw + drop your shoulders

- Step outside for 3 deep breaths

- Name three things supporting you today

Daily Evening Reflection Pages

(For emotional processing + nervous system unwinding)

Where did stress show up today?

Body: _____

Mind: _____

Emotions: _____

How did I respond?

☐ Reacted quickly
☐ Shut down
☐ Over-functioned
☐ Avoided
☐ Paused
☐ Responded intentionally

Notes:

_____
_____
_____

What part of me needed more care?

_____
_____
_____
_____

A moment I'm proud of today:
_____
_____
_____
_____
_____

Something I want to release tonight:
_____
_____
_____
_____
_____

Notes:
_____
_____
_____

Closing breath cue:

Inhale for 4, hold for 2, exhale for 6 — repeat 3 times.

| JAN | FEB | MAR | APR | MAY | JUN | JUL | AUG | SEP | OCT | NOV | DEC |

1 2 3 4 5 6 7 8 9 10 11 12 13 14 15 16 17 18 19 20 21 22 23 24 25 26 27 28 29 30 31

Daily Morning Reset
(For mental clarity + emotional grounding)

Today, my body feels…

☐ Tense
☐ Rested
☐ Scattered
☐ Heavy
☐ Neutral
☐ Something else: _____

One thing weighing on me today is…

_____
_____
_____
_____

Emotion I'm carrying into today:

_____
_____
_____
_____

What I need emotionally right now:

☐ Space
☐ Encouragement
☐ Boundaries
☐ Rest
☐ Focus
☐ Connection
☐ Other: _____

My intention for today:
A sentence or two that feels doable, gentle, and honest.

_____
_____
_____

A micro-practice to begin the day:
(Choose one)

- 1-minute grounding breath

- Soften your jaw + drop your shoulders

- Step outside for 3 deep breaths

- Name three things supporting you today

Daily Evening Reflection Pages
(For emotional processing + nervous system unwinding)

Where did stress show up today?

Body: _____
Mind: _____
Emotions: _____

How did I respond?

☐ Reacted quickly
☐ Shut down
☐ Over-functioned
☐ Avoided
☐ Paused
☐ Responded intentionally

Notes:
_____
_____
_____

What part of me needed more care?

_____
_____
_____
_____

A moment I'm proud of today:
_____
_____
_____
_____
_____
_____

Something I want to release tonight:
_____
_____
_____
_____
_____
_____

Notes:
_____
_____
_____

Closing breath cue:

Inhale for 4, hold for 2, exhale for 6 — repeat 3 times.

JAN	FEB	MAR	APR	MAY	JUN	JUL	AUG	SEP	OCT	NOV	DEC

1 2 3 4 5 6 7 8 9 10 11 12 13 14 15 16 17 18 19 20 21 22 23 24 25 26 27 28 29 30 31

Daily Morning Reset

(For mental clarity + emotional grounding)

Today, my body feels…

☐ Tense
☐ Rested
☐ Scattered
☐ Heavy
☐ Neutral
☐ Something else: _____

One thing weighing on me today is…

_____
_____
_____
_____
_____

Emotion I'm carrying into today:

_____
_____
_____
_____
_____

What I need emotionally right now:

- ☐ Space
- ☐ Encouragement
- ☐ Boundaries
- ☐ Rest
- ☐ Focus
- ☐ Connection
- ☐ Other: _____

My intention for today:

A sentence or two that feels doable, gentle, and honest.

_____
_____
_____

A micro-practice to begin the day:

(Choose one)

- 1-minute grounding breath

- Soften your jaw + drop your shoulders

- Step outside for 3 deep breaths

- Name three things supporting you today

Daily Evening Reflection Pages
(For emotional processing + nervous system unwinding)

Where did stress show up today?

Body: _____
Mind: _____
Emotions: _____

How did I respond?

☐ Reacted quickly
☐ Shut down
☐ Over-functioned
☐ Avoided
☐ Paused
☐ Responded intentionally

Notes:
_____
_____
_____

What part of me needed more care?

_____
_____
_____
_____

A moment I'm proud of today:
_____
_____
_____
_____
_____

Something I want to release tonight:
_____
_____
_____
_____
_____

Notes:
_____
_____
_____

Closing breath cue:

Inhale for 4, hold for 2, exhale for 6 — repeat 3 times.

| JAN | FEB | MAR | APR | MAY | JUN | JUL | AUG | SEP | OCT | NOV | DEC |

1 2 3 4 5 6 7 8 9 10 11 12 13 14 15 16 17 18 19 20 21 22 23 24 25 26 27 28 29 30 31

Daily Morning Reset
(For mental clarity + emotional grounding)

Today, my body feels…

- ☐ Tense
- ☐ Rested
- ☐ Scattered
- ☐ Heavy
- ☐ Neutral
- ☐ Something else: _____

One thing weighing on me today is…

_____
_____
_____
_____
_____

Emotion I'm carrying into today:

_____
_____
_____
_____
_____

What I need emotionally right now:
- ☐ Space
- ☐ Encouragement
- ☐ Boundaries
- ☐ Rest
- ☐ Focus
- ☐ Connection
- ☐ Other: _____

My intention for today:
A sentence or two that feels doable, gentle, and honest.

_____
_____
_____

A micro-practice to begin the day:
(Choose one)

- 1-minute grounding breath

- Soften your jaw + drop your shoulders

- Step outside for 3 deep breaths

- Name three things supporting you today

Daily Evening Reflection Pages
(For emotional processing + nervous system unwinding)

Where did stress show up today?

Body: _____
Mind: _____
Emotions: _____

How did I respond?

☐ Reacted quickly
☐ Shut down
☐ Over-functioned
☐ Avoided
☐ Paused
☐ Responded intentionally

Notes:
_____
_____
_____

What part of me needed more care?

_____
_____
_____
_____

A moment I'm proud of today:
_____
_____
_____
_____
_____

Something I want to release tonight:
_____
_____
_____
_____
_____

Notes:
_____
_____

Closing breath cue:
Inhale for 4, hold for 2, exhale for 6 — repeat 3 times.

JAN	FEB	MAR	APR	MAY	JUN	JUL	AUG	SEP	OCT	NOV	DEC

1 2 3 4 5 6 7 8 9 10 11 12 13 14 15 16 17 18 19 20 21 22 23 24 25 26 27 28 29 30 31

Daily Morning Reset
(For mental clarity + emotional grounding)

Today, my body feels…

☐ Tense
☐ Rested
☐ Scattered
☐ Heavy
☐ Neutral
☐ Something else: _____

One thing weighing on me today is…

_____
_____
_____
_____
_____

Emotion I'm carrying into today:

_____
_____
_____
_____
_____

What I need emotionally right now:

☐ Space
☐ Encouragement
☐ Boundaries
☐ Rest
☐ Focus
☐ Connection
☐ Other: _____

My intention for today:
A sentence or two that feels doable, gentle, and honest.

_____
_____
_____

A micro-practice to begin the day:
(Choose one)

- 1-minute grounding breath

- Soften your jaw + drop your shoulders

- Step outside for 3 deep breaths

- Name three things supporting you today

Daily Evening Reflection Pages
(For emotional processing + nervous system unwinding)

Where did stress show up today?

Body: _____
Mind: _____
Emotions: _____

How did I respond?

- ☐ Reacted quickly
- ☐ Shut down
- ☐ Over-functioned
- ☐ Avoided
- ☐ Paused
- ☐ Responded intentionally

Notes:
_____
_____
_____

What part of me needed more care?

_____
_____
_____

A moment I'm proud of today:
_____
_____
_____
_____
_____

Something I want to release tonight:
_____
_____
_____
_____
_____

Notes:
_____
_____
_____

Closing breath cue:

Inhale for 4, hold for 2, exhale for 6 — repeat 3 times.

Weekly Reflection

Energy Check-In

What drained me this week?

_____
_____
_____

What restored me this week?

_____
_____
_____

Emotional Patterns I Noticed

- When did I override myself?

- When did I honor my capacity?

- What emotion repeated most?

Notes:
_____
_____

A boundary I need for next week:
_____
_____

One small shift that would support me next week:
_____
_____

Weekly Stress Pattern Awareness Worksheet

What My Stress Cycle This Week Looked Like:

Trigger → Reaction → Emotion → Behavior → Aftermath

Trigger: _____   Trigger: _____   Trigger: _____
Reaction: _____   Reaction: _____   Reaction: _____
Emotion: _____   Emotion: _____   Emotion: _____
Behavior: _____   Behavior: _____   Behavior: _____
Aftermath: _____   Aftermath: _____   Aftermath: _____

What my body did under stress:

- ☐ Tight chest
- ☐ Stomach tension
- ☐ Shallow breathing
- ☐ Head pressure
- ☐ Frozen / shut down
- ☐ Other: _____

What I needed in those moments:

- ☐ Slowness
- ☐ Clarity
- ☐ Space
- ☐ Reassurance
- ☐ Regulation
- ☐ Boundaries

Notes:

_____
_____

JAN　FEB　MAR　APR　MAY　JUN　JUL　AUG　SEP　OCT　NOV　DEC
1　2　3　4　5　6　7　8　9　10　11　12　13　14　15　16　17　18　19　20　21　22　23　24　25　26　27　28　29　30　31

Daily Morning Reset

(For mental clarity + emotional grounding)

Today, my body feels…

- ☐ Tense
- ☐ Rested
- ☐ Scattered
- ☐ Heavy
- ☐ Neutral
- ☐ Something else: _____

One thing weighing on me today is…

_____
_____
_____
_____
_____

Emotion I'm carrying into today:

_____
_____
_____
_____

What I need emotionally right now:

☐ Space
☐ Encouragement
☐ Boundaries
☐ Rest
☐ Focus
☐ Connection
☐ Other: _____

My intention for today:
A sentence or two that feels doable, gentle, and honest.

_____
_____
_____

A micro-practice to begin the day:
(Choose one)

- 1-minute grounding breath

- Soften your jaw + drop your shoulders

- Step outside for 3 deep breaths

- Name three things supporting you today

Daily Evening Reflection Pages
(For emotional processing + nervous system unwinding)

Where did stress show up today?

Body: _____
Mind: _____
Emotions: _____

How did I respond?

☐ Reacted quickly
☐ Shut down
☐ Over-functioned
☐ Avoided
☐ Paused
☐ Responded intentionally

Notes:
_____
_____
_____

What part of me needed more care?

_____
_____
_____
_____

A moment I'm proud of today:
_____
_____
_____
_____
_____

Something I want to release tonight:
_____
_____
_____
_____
_____

Notes:
_____
_____
_____

Closing breath cue:

Inhale for 4, hold for 2, exhale for 6 — repeat 3 times.

JAN FEB MAR APR MAY JUN JUL AUG SEP OCT NOV DEC
1 2 3 4 5 6 7 8 9 10 11 12 13 14 15 16 17 18 19 20 21 22 23 24 25 26 27 28 29 30 31

Daily Morning Reset
(For mental clarity + emotional grounding)

Today, my body feels...

☐ Tense
☐ Rested
☐ Scattered
☐ Heavy
☐ Neutral
☐ Something else: _____

One thing weighing on me today is...

_____
_____
_____
_____
_____

Emotion I'm carrying into today:

_____
_____
_____
_____
_____

What I need emotionally right now:

☐ Space
☐ Encouragement
☐ Boundaries
☐ Rest
☐ Focus
☐ Connection
☐ Other: _____

My intention for today:
A sentence or two that feels doable, gentle, and honest.

_____
_____
_____

A micro-practice to begin the day:
(Choose one)

- 1-minute grounding breath

- Soften your jaw + drop your shoulders

- Step outside for 3 deep breaths

- Name three things supporting you today

Daily Evening Reflection Pages
(For emotional processing + nervous system unwinding)

Where did stress show up today?

Body: _____

Mind: _____

Emotions: _____

How did I respond?

☐ Reacted quickly
☐ Shut down
☐ Over-functioned
☐ Avoided
☐ Paused
☐ Responded intentionally

Notes:
_____
_____
_____

What part of me needed more care?
_____
_____
_____
_____

A moment I'm proud of today:

_____
_____
_____
_____
_____

Something I want to release tonight:

_____
_____
_____
_____
_____

Notes:

_____
_____
_____

Closing breath cue:

Inhale for 4, hold for 2, exhale for 6 — repeat 3 times.

JAN	FEB	MAR	APR	MAY	JUN	JUL	AUG	SEP	OCT	NOV	DEC

1 2 3 4 5 6 7 8 9 10 11 12 13 14 15 16 17 18 19 20 21 22 23 24 25 26 27 28 29 30 31

Daily Morning Reset
(For mental clarity + emotional grounding)

Today, my body feels...

☐ Tense
☐ Rested
☐ Scattered
☐ Heavy
☐ Neutral
☐ Something else: _____

One thing weighing on me today is...

_____
_____
_____
_____

Emotion I'm carrying into today:

_____
_____
_____
_____

What I need emotionally right now:

☐ Space
☐ Encouragement
☐ Boundaries
☐ Rest
☐ Focus
☐ Connection
☐ Other: _____

My intention for today:
A sentence or two that feels doable, gentle, and honest.

_____
_____
_____

A micro-practice to begin the day:
(Choose one)

- 1-minute grounding breath

- Soften your jaw + drop your shoulders

- Step outside for 3 deep breaths

- Name three things supporting you today

Daily Evening Reflection Pages
(For emotional processing + nervous system unwinding)

Where did stress show up today?

Body: _____
Mind: _____
Emotions: _____

How did I respond?

☐ Reacted quickly
☐ Shut down
☐ Over-functioned
☐ Avoided
☐ Paused
☐ Responded intentionally

Notes:
_____
_____
_____

What part of me needed more care?

_____
_____
_____

A moment I'm proud of today:
_____
_____
_____
_____
_____

Something I want to release tonight:
_____
_____
_____
_____
_____

Notes:
_____
_____
_____

Closing breath cue:

Inhale for 4, hold for 2, exhale for 6 — repeat 3 times.

JAN FEB MAR APR MAY JUN JUL AUG SEP OCT NOV DEC
1 2 3 4 5 6 7 8 9 10 11 12 13 14 15 16 17 18 19 20 21 22 23 24 25 26 27 28 29 30 31

Daily Morning Reset

(For mental clarity + emotional grounding)

Today, my body feels...

☐ Tense
☐ Rested
☐ Scattered
☐ Heavy
☐ Neutral
☐ Something else: _____

One thing weighing on me today is...

_____
_____
_____
_____

Emotion I'm carrying into today:

_____
_____
_____
_____

What I need emotionally right now:

- ☐ Space
- ☐ Encouragement
- ☐ Boundaries
- ☐ Rest
- ☐ Focus
- ☐ Connection
- ☐ Other: _____

My intention for today:

A sentence or two that feels doable, gentle, and honest.

_____
_____
_____

A micro-practice to begin the day:

(Choose one)

- 1-minute grounding breath

- Soften your jaw + drop your shoulders

- Step outside for 3 deep breaths

- Name three things supporting you today

Daily Evening Reflection Pages
(For emotional processing + nervous system unwinding)

Where did stress show up today?

Body: _____
Mind: _____
Emotions: _____

How did I respond?

☐ Reacted quickly
☐ Shut down
☐ Over-functioned
☐ Avoided
☐ Paused
☐ Responded intentionally

Notes:
_____
_____
_____

What part of me needed more care?

_____
_____
_____
_____

A moment I'm proud of today:
_____
_____
_____
_____
_____

Something I want to release tonight:
_____
_____
_____
_____
_____

Notes:
_____
_____
_____

Closing breath cue:

Inhale for 4, hold for 2, exhale for 6 — repeat 3 times.

| JAN | FEB | MAR | APR | MAY | JUN | JUL | AUG | SEP | OCT | NOV | DEC |

1 2 3 4 5 6 7 8 9 10 11 12 13 14 15 16 17 18 19 20 21 22 23 24 25 26 27 28 29 30 31

Daily Morning Reset
(For mental clarity + emotional grounding)

Today, my body feels…

☐ Tense
☐ Rested
☐ Scattered
☐ Heavy
☐ Neutral
☐ Something else: _____

One thing weighing on me today is…

_____
_____
_____
_____

Emotion I'm carrying into today:

_____
_____
_____
_____

What I need emotionally right now:

- ☐ Space
- ☐ Encouragement
- ☐ Boundaries
- ☐ Rest
- ☐ Focus
- ☐ Connection
- ☐ Other: _____

My intention for today:

A sentence or two that feels doable, gentle, and honest.

_____
_____
_____

A micro-practice to begin the day:

(Choose one)

- 1-minute grounding breath

- Soften your jaw + drop your shoulders

- Step outside for 3 deep breaths

- Name three things supporting you today

Daily Evening Reflection Pages
(For emotional processing + nervous system unwinding)

Where did stress show up today?

Body: _____
Mind: _____
Emotions: _____

How did I respond?

- ☐ Reacted quickly
- ☐ Shut down
- ☐ Over-functioned
- ☐ Avoided
- ☐ Paused
- ☐ Responded intentionally

Notes:
_____
_____
_____

What part of me needed more care?

_____
_____
_____
_____

A moment I'm proud of today:
_____
_____
_____
_____
_____

Something I want to release tonight:
_____
_____
_____
_____
_____

Notes:
_____
_____
_____

Closing breath cue:

Inhale for 4, hold for 2, exhale for 6 — repeat 3 times.

JAN　FEB　MAR　APR　MAY　JUN　JUL　AUG　SEP　OCT　NOV　DEC
1　2　3　4　5　6　7　8　9　10　11　12　13　14　15　16　17　18　19　20　21　22　23　24　25　26　27　28　29　30　31

Daily Morning Reset

(For mental clarity + emotional grounding)

Today, my body feels…

- ☐ Tense
- ☐ Rested
- ☐ Scattered
- ☐ Heavy
- ☐ Neutral
- ☐ Something else: _____

One thing weighing on me today is…

_____
_____
_____
_____
_____

Emotion I'm carrying into today:

_____
_____
_____
_____

What I need emotionally right now:

☐ Space
☐ Encouragement
☐ Boundaries
☐ Rest
☐ Focus
☐ Connection
☐ Other: _____

My intention for today:
A sentence or two that feels doable, gentle, and honest.

_____
_____
_____

A micro-practice to begin the day:
(Choose one)

- 1-minute grounding breath

- Soften your jaw + drop your shoulders

- Step outside for 3 deep breaths

- Name three things supporting you today

Daily Evening Reflection Pages
(For emotional processing + nervous system unwinding)

Where did stress show up today?

Body: _____
Mind: _____
Emotions: _____

How did I respond?

☐ Reacted quickly
☐ Shut down
☐ Over-functioned
☐ Avoided
☐ Paused
☐ Responded intentionally

Notes:
_____
_____
_____

What part of me needed more care?
_____
_____
_____
_____

A moment I'm proud of today:
_____
_____
_____
_____
_____
_____

Something I want to release tonight:
_____
_____
_____
_____
_____
_____

Notes:
_____
_____
_____

Closing breath cue:

Inhale for 4, hold for 2, exhale for 6 — repeat 3 times.

| JAN | FEB | MAR | APR | MAY | JUN | JUL | AUG | SEP | OCT | NOV | DEC |

1 2 3 4 5 6 7 8 9 10 11 12 13 14 15 16 17 18 19 20 21 22 23 24 25 26 27 28 29 30 31

Daily Morning Reset

(For mental clarity + emotional grounding)

Today, my body feels…

- ☐ Tense
- ☐ Rested
- ☐ Scattered
- ☐ Heavy
- ☐ Neutral
- ☐ Something else: _____

One thing weighing on me today is…

_____
_____
_____
_____
_____

Emotion I'm carrying into today:

_____
_____
_____
_____
_____

What I need emotionally right now:

☐ Space
☐ Encouragement
☐ Boundaries
☐ Rest
☐ Focus
☐ Connection
☐ Other: _____

My intention for today:
A sentence or two that feels doable, gentle, and honest.

_____
_____
_____

A micro-practice to begin the day:
(Choose one)

- 1-minute grounding breath

- Soften your jaw + drop your shoulders

- Step outside for 3 deep breaths

- Name three things supporting you today

Daily Evening Reflection Pages
(For emotional processing + nervous system unwinding)

Where did stress show up today?

Body: _____
Mind: _____
Emotions: _____

How did I respond?

☐ Reacted quickly
☐ Shut down
☐ Over-functioned
☐ Avoided
☐ Paused
☐ Responded intentionally

Notes:
_____
_____
_____

What part of me needed more care?
_____
_____
_____
_____

A moment I'm proud of today:
_____
_____
_____
_____
_____

Something I want to release tonight:
_____
_____
_____
_____
_____

Notes:
_____
_____
_____

Closing breath cue:

Inhale for 4, hold for 2, exhale for 6 — repeat 3 times.

Weekly Reflection

Energy Check-In

What drained me this week?

_____
_____
_____

What restored me this week?

_____
_____
_____

Emotional Patterns I Noticed

- When did I override myself?

- When did I honor my capacity?

- What emotion repeated most?

Notes:

_____
_____

A boundary I need for next week:

_____
_____

One small shift that would support me next week:

_____
_____

Weekly Stress Pattern Awareness Worksheet

What My Stress Cycle This Week Looked Like:

Trigger → Reaction → Emotion → Behavior → Aftermath

Trigger: _____ Trigger: _____ Trigger: _____
Reaction: _____ Reaction: _____ Reaction: _____
Emotion: _____ Emotion: _____ Emotion: _____
Behavior: _____ Behavior: _____ Behavior: _____
Aftermath: _____ Aftermath: _____ Aftermath: _____

What my body did under stress:

☐ Tight chest
☐ Stomach tension
☐ Shallow breathing
☐ Head pressure
☐ Frozen / shut down
☐ Other: _____

What I needed in those moments:

☐ Slowness
☐ Clarity
☐ Space
☐ Reassurance
☐ Regulation
☐ Boundaries

Notes:

_____
_____

JAN	FEB	MAR	APR	MAY	JUN	JUL	AUG	SEP	OCT	NOV	DEC

1 2 3 4 5 6 7 8 9 10 11 12 13 14 15 16 17 18 19 20 21 22 23 24 25 26 27 28 29 30 31

Daily Morning Reset
(For mental clarity + emotional grounding)

Today, my body feels...

☐ Tense
☐ Rested
☐ Scattered
☐ Heavy
☐ Neutral
☐ Something else: _____

One thing weighing on me today is...

_____
_____
_____
_____
_____

Emotion I'm carrying into today:

_____
_____
_____
_____

What I need emotionally right now:

☐ Space
☐ Encouragement
☐ Boundaries
☐ Rest
☐ Focus
☐ Connection
☐ Other: _____

My intention for today:
A sentence or two that feels doable, gentle, and honest.

_____
_____
_____

A micro-practice to begin the day:
(Choose one)

- 1-minute grounding breath

- Soften your jaw + drop your shoulders

- Step outside for 3 deep breaths

- Name three things supporting you today

Daily Evening Reflection Pages
(For emotional processing + nervous system unwinding)

Where did stress show up today?

Body: _____
Mind: _____
Emotions: _____

How did I respond?

☐ Reacted quickly
☐ Shut down
☐ Over-functioned
☐ Avoided
☐ Paused
☐ Responded intentionally

Notes:
_____
_____
_____

What part of me needed more care?
_____
_____
_____

A moment I'm proud of today:
_____
_____
_____
_____
_____
_____

Something I want to release tonight:
_____
_____
_____
_____
_____
_____

Notes:
_____
_____
_____

Closing breath cue:
Inhale for 4, hold for 2, exhale for 6 — repeat 3 times.

JAN	FEB	MAR	APR	MAY	JUN	JUL	AUG	SEP	OCT	NOV	DEC

1 2 3 4 5 6 7 8 9 10 11 12 13 14 15 16 17 18 19 20 21 22 23 24 25 26 27 28 29 30 31

Daily Morning Reset
(For mental clarity + emotional grounding)

Today, my body feels…

☐ Tense
☐ Rested
☐ Scattered
☐ Heavy
☐ Neutral
☐ Something else: _____

One thing weighing on me today is…

_____
_____
_____
_____
_____

Emotion I'm carrying into today:

_____
_____
_____
_____

What I need emotionally right now:

☐ Space
☐ Encouragement
☐ Boundaries
☐ Rest
☐ Focus
☐ Connection
☐ Other: _____

My intention for today:
A sentence or two that feels doable, gentle, and honest.

_____
_____
_____

A micro-practice to begin the day:
(Choose one)

- 1-minute grounding breath

- Soften your jaw + drop your shoulders

- Step outside for 3 deep breaths

- Name three things supporting you today

Daily Evening Reflection Pages
(For emotional processing + nervous system unwinding)

Where did stress show up today?

Body: _____
Mind: _____
Emotions: _____

How did I respond?

- ☐ Reacted quickly
- ☐ Shut down
- ☐ Over-functioned
- ☐ Avoided
- ☐ Paused
- ☐ Responded intentionally

Notes:
_____
_____
_____

What part of me needed more care?

_____
_____
_____
_____

A moment I'm proud of today:
_____
_____
_____
_____
_____

Something I want to release tonight:
_____
_____
_____
_____
_____

Notes:
_____
_____
_____

Closing breath cue:

Inhale for 4, hold for 2, exhale for 6 — repeat 3 times.

JAN	FEB	MAR	APR	MAY	JUN	JUL	AUG	SEP	OCT	NOV	DEC

1 2 3 4 5 6 7 8 9 10 11 12 13 14 15 16 17 18 19 20 21 22 23 24 25 26 27 28 29 30 31

Daily Morning Reset

(For mental clarity + emotional grounding)

Today, my body feels...

☐ Tense
☐ Rested
☐ Scattered
☐ Heavy
☐ Neutral
☐ Something else: _____

One thing weighing on me today is...

_____
_____
_____
_____
_____

Emotion I'm carrying into today:

_____
_____
_____
_____
_____

What I need emotionally right now:

☐ Space
☐ Encouragement
☐ Boundaries
☐ Rest
☐ Focus
☐ Connection
☐ Other: _____

My intention for today:
A sentence or two that feels doable, gentle, and honest.

_____
_____
_____

A micro-practice to begin the day:
(Choose one)

- 1-minute grounding breath

- Soften your jaw + drop your shoulders

- Step outside for 3 deep breaths

- Name three things supporting you today

Daily Evening Reflection Pages
(For emotional processing + nervous system unwinding)

Where did stress show up today?

Body: _____

Mind: _____

Emotions: _____

How did I respond?

- ☐ Reacted quickly
- ☐ Shut down
- ☐ Over-functioned
- ☐ Avoided
- ☐ Paused
- ☐ Responded intentionally

Notes:
_____
_____
_____

What part of me needed more care?
_____
_____
_____
_____

A moment I'm proud of today:
_____
_____
_____
_____

Something I want to release tonight:
_____
_____
_____
_____
_____

Notes:
_____
_____

Closing breath cue:

Inhale for 4, hold for 2, exhale for 6 — repeat 3 times.

JAN	FEB	MAR	APR	MAY	JUN	JUL	AUG	SEP	OCT	NOV	DEC

1 2 3 4 5 6 7 8 9 10 11 12 13 14 15 16 17 18 19 20 21 22 23 24 25 26 27 28 29 30 31

Daily Morning Reset
(For mental clarity + emotional grounding)

Today, my body feels...

☐ Tense
☐ Rested
☐ Scattered
☐ Heavy
☐ Neutral
☐ Something else: _____

One thing weighing on me today is...

_____
_____
_____
_____
_____

Emotion I'm carrying into today:

_____
_____
_____
_____
_____

What I need emotionally right now:

☐ Space
☐ Encouragement
☐ Boundaries
☐ Rest
☐ Focus
☐ Connection
☐ Other: _____

My intention for today:
A sentence or two that feels doable, gentle, and honest.

_____
_____
_____

A micro-practice to begin the day:
(Choose one)

- 1-minute grounding breath

- Soften your jaw + drop your shoulders

- Step outside for 3 deep breaths

- Name three things supporting you today

Daily Evening Reflection Pages
(For emotional processing + nervous system unwinding)

Where did stress show up today?

Body: _____
Mind: _____
Emotions: _____

How did I respond?

☐ Reacted quickly
☐ Shut down
☐ Over-functioned
☐ Avoided
☐ Paused
☐ Responded intentionally

Notes:
_____
_____
_____

What part of me needed more care?
_____
_____
_____
_____

A moment I'm proud of today:
_____
_____
_____
_____
_____

Something I want to release tonight:
_____
_____
_____
_____
_____

Notes:
_____
_____
_____

Closing breath cue:

Inhale for 4, hold for 2, exhale for 6 — repeat 3 times.

JAN FEB MAR APR MAY JUN JUL AUG SEP OCT NOV DEC
1 2 3 4 5 6 7 8 9 10 11 12 13 14 15 16 17 18 19 20 21 22 23 24 25 26 27 28 29 30 31

Daily Morning Reset
(For mental clarity + emotional grounding)

Today, my body feels...

- ☐ Tense
- ☐ Rested
- ☐ Scattered
- ☐ Heavy
- ☐ Neutral
- ☐ Something else: _____

One thing weighing on me today is...

_____
_____
_____
_____
_____

Emotion I'm carrying into today:

_____
_____
_____
_____
_____

What I need emotionally right now:

☐ Space
☐ Encouragement
☐ Boundaries
☐ Rest
☐ Focus
☐ Connection
☐ Other: _____

My intention for today:

A sentence or two that feels doable, gentle, and honest.

_____
_____
_____

A micro-practice to begin the day:
(Choose one)

- 1-minute grounding breath

- Soften your jaw + drop your shoulders

- Step outside for 3 deep breaths

- Name three things supporting you today

Daily Evening Reflection Pages
(For emotional processing + nervous system unwinding)

Where did stress show up today?

Body: _____
Mind: _____
Emotions: _____

How did I respond?

☐ Reacted quickly
☐ Shut down
☐ Over-functioned
☐ Avoided
☐ Paused
☐ Responded intentionally

Notes:
_____
_____
_____

What part of me needed more care?
_____
_____
_____
_____

A moment I'm proud of today:
_____
_____
_____
_____
_____

Something I want to release tonight:
_____
_____
_____
_____
_____

Notes:
_____
_____
_____

Closing breath cue:

Inhale for 4, hold for 2, exhale for 6 — repeat 3 times.

JAN FEB MAR APR MAY JUN JUL AUG SEP OCT NOV DEC
1 2 3 4 5 6 7 8 9 10 11 12 13 14 15 16 17 18 19 20 21 22 23 24 25 26 27 28 29 30 31

Daily Morning Reset
(For mental clarity + emotional grounding)

Today, my body feels...
- ☐ Tense
- ☐ Rested
- ☐ Scattered
- ☐ Heavy
- ☐ Neutral
- ☐ Something else: _____

One thing weighing on me today is...

_____
_____
_____
_____

Emotion I'm carrying into today:

_____
_____
_____
_____

What I need emotionally right now:

☐ Space
☐ Encouragement
☐ Boundaries
☐ Rest
☐ Focus
☐ Connection
☐ Other: _____

My intention for today:
A sentence or two that feels doable, gentle, and honest.

_____
_____
_____

A micro-practice to begin the day:
(Choose one)

- 1-minute grounding breath

- Soften your jaw + drop your shoulders

- Step outside for 3 deep breaths

- Name three things supporting you today

Daily Evening Reflection Pages
(For emotional processing + nervous system unwinding)

Where did stress show up today?

Body: _____
Mind: _____
Emotions: _____

How did I respond?

☐ Reacted quickly
☐ Shut down
☐ Over-functioned
☐ Avoided
☐ Paused
☐ Responded intentionally

Notes:
_____
_____
_____

What part of me needed more care?
_____
_____
_____

A moment I'm proud of today:
_____
_____
_____
_____
_____

Something I want to release tonight:
_____
_____
_____
_____
_____
_____

Notes:
_____
_____
_____

Closing breath cue:

Inhale for 4, hold for 2, exhale for 6 — repeat 3 times.

JAN	FEB	MAR	APR	MAY	JUN	JUL	AUG	SEP	OCT	NOV	DEC

1 2 3 4 5 6 7 8 9 10 11 12 13 14 15 16 17 18 19 20 21 22 23 24 25 26 27 28 29 30 31

Daily Morning Reset
(For mental clarity + emotional grounding)

Today, my body feels…

- ☐ Tense
- ☐ Rested
- ☐ Scattered
- ☐ Heavy
- ☐ Neutral
- ☐ Something else: _____

One thing weighing on me today is…

_____
_____
_____
_____
_____

Emotion I'm carrying into today:

_____
_____
_____
_____
_____

What I need emotionally right now:

☐ Space
☐ Encouragement
☐ Boundaries
☐ Rest
☐ Focus
☐ Connection
☐ Other: _____

My intention for today:
A sentence or two that feels doable, gentle, and honest.

_____
_____
_____

A micro-practice to begin the day:
(Choose one)

- 1-minute grounding breath

- Soften your jaw + drop your shoulders

- Step outside for 3 deep breaths

- Name three things supporting you today

Daily Evening Reflection Pages
(For emotional processing + nervous system unwinding)

Where did stress show up today?

Body: _____
Mind: _____
Emotions: _____

How did I respond?

☐ Reacted quickly
☐ Shut down
☐ Over-functioned
☐ Avoided
☐ Paused
☐ Responded intentionally

Notes:
_____
_____
_____

What part of me needed more care?

_____
_____
_____

A moment I'm proud of today:
_____
_____
_____
_____
_____

Something I want to release tonight:
_____
_____
_____
_____
_____

Notes:
_____
_____
_____

Closing breath cue:

Inhale for 4, hold for 2, exhale for 6 — repeat 3 times.

Weekly Reflection

Energy Check-In

What drained me this week?

_____
_____
_____

What restored me this week?

_____
_____
_____

Emotional Patterns I Noticed

- When did I override myself?

- When did I honor my capacity?

- What emotion repeated most?

Notes:
_____
_____

A boundary I need for next week:
_____
_____

One small shift that would support me next week:
_____
_____

Weekly Stress Pattern Awareness Worksheet

What My Stress Cycle This Week Looked Like:

Trigger → Reaction → Emotion → Behavior → Aftermath

Trigger: _____   Trigger: _____   Trigger: _____
Reaction: _____   Reaction: _____   Reaction: _____
Emotion: _____   Emotion: _____   Emotion: _____
Behavior: _____   Behavior: _____   Behavior: _____
Aftermath: _____   Aftermath: _____   Aftermath: _____

What my body did under stress:

- ☐ Tight chest
- ☐ Stomach tension
- ☐ Shallow breathing
- ☐ Head pressure
- ☐ Frozen / shut down
- ☐ Other: _____

What I needed in those moments:

- ☐ Slowness
- ☐ Clarity
- ☐ Space
- ☐ Reassurance
- ☐ Regulation
- ☐ Boundaries

Notes:
_____
_____

JAN　FEB　MAR　APR　MAY　JUN　JUL　AUG　SEP　OCT　NOV　DEC
1　2　3　4　5　6　7　8　9　10　11　12　13　14　15　16　17　18　19　20　21　22　23　24　25　26　27　28　29　30　31

Daily Morning Reset

(For mental clarity + emotional grounding)

Today, my body feels...

- ☐ Tense
- ☐ Rested
- ☐ Scattered
- ☐ Heavy
- ☐ Neutral
- ☐ Something else: _____

One thing weighing on me today is...

_____
_____
_____
_____
_____

Emotion I'm carrying into today:

_____
_____
_____
_____

What I need emotionally right now:

☐ Space
☐ Encouragement
☐ Boundaries
☐ Rest
☐ Focus
☐ Connection
☐ Other: _____

My intention for today:
A sentence or two that feels doable, gentle, and honest.

_____
_____
_____

A micro-practice to begin the day:
(Choose one)

- 1-minute grounding breath

- Soften your jaw + drop your shoulders

- Step outside for 3 deep breaths

- Name three things supporting you today

Daily Evening Reflection Pages
(For emotional processing + nervous system unwinding)

Where did stress show up today?

Body: _____
Mind: _____
Emotions: _____

How did I respond?

☐ Reacted quickly
☐ Shut down
☐ Over-functioned
☐ Avoided
☐ Paused
☐ Responded intentionally

Notes:
_____
_____
_____

What part of me needed more care?

_____
_____
_____
_____

A moment I'm proud of today:
_____
_____
_____
_____
_____

Something I want to release tonight:
_____
_____
_____
_____
_____

Notes:
_____
_____
_____

Closing breath cue:

Inhale for 4, hold for 2, exhale for 6 — repeat 3 times.

JAN	FEB	MAR	APR	MAY	JUN	JUL	AUG	SEP	OCT	NOV	DEC

1 2 3 4 5 6 7 8 9 10 11 12 13 14 15 16 17 18 19 20 21 22 23 24 25 26 27 28 29 30 31

Daily Morning Reset
(For mental clarity + emotional grounding)

Today, my body feels…

☐ Tense
☐ Rested
☐ Scattered
☐ Heavy
☐ Neutral
☐ Something else: _____

One thing weighing on me today is…

_____
_____
_____
_____
_____

Emotion I'm carrying into today:

_____
_____
_____
_____
_____

What I need emotionally right now:

☐ Space
☐ Encouragement
☐ Boundaries
☐ Rest
☐ Focus
☐ Connection
☐ Other: _____

My intention for today:
A sentence or two that feels doable, gentle, and honest.

_____
_____
_____

A micro-practice to begin the day:
(Choose one)

- 1-minute grounding breath

- Soften your jaw + drop your shoulders

- Step outside for 3 deep breaths

- Name three things supporting you today

Daily Evening Reflection Pages
(For emotional processing + nervous system unwinding)

Where did stress show up today?

Body: _____
Mind: _____
Emotions: _____

How did I respond?

- ☐ Reacted quickly
- ☐ Shut down
- ☐ Over-functioned
- ☐ Avoided
- ☐ Paused
- ☐ Responded intentionally

Notes:
_____
_____
_____

What part of me needed more care?

_____
_____
_____
_____

A moment I'm proud of today:
_____
_____
_____
_____
_____

Something I want to release tonight:
_____
_____
_____
_____
_____

Notes:
_____
_____
_____

Closing breath cue:

Inhale for 4, hold for 2, exhale for 6 — repeat 3 times.

JAN	FEB	MAR	APR	MAY	JUN	JUL	AUG	SEP	OCT	NOV	DEC

1 2 3 4 5 6 7 8 9 10 11 12 13 14 15 16 17 18 19 20 21 22 23 24 25 26 27 28 29 30 31

Daily Morning Reset
(For mental clarity + emotional grounding)

Today, my body feels...

☐ Tense
☐ Rested
☐ Scattered
☐ Heavy
☐ Neutral
☐ Something else: _____

One thing weighing on me today is...

_____
_____
_____
_____
_____

Emotion I'm carrying into today:

_____
_____
_____
_____
_____

What I need emotionally right now:

☐ Space
☐ Encouragement
☐ Boundaries
☐ Rest
☐ Focus
☐ Connection
☐ Other: _____

My intention for today:
A sentence or two that feels doable, gentle, and honest.

_____
_____
_____

A micro-practice to begin the day:
(Choose one)

- 1-minute grounding breath

- Soften your jaw + drop your shoulders

- Step outside for 3 deep breaths

- Name three things supporting you today

Daily Evening Reflection Pages
(For emotional processing + nervous system unwinding)

Where did stress show up today?

Body: _____

Mind: _____

Emotions: _____

How did I respond?

☐ Reacted quickly
☐ Shut down
☐ Over-functioned
☐ Avoided
☐ Paused
☐ Responded intentionally

Notes:
_____
_____
_____

What part of me needed more care?

_____
_____
_____
_____

A moment I'm proud of today:
_____
_____
_____
_____
_____

Something I want to release tonight:
_____
_____
_____
_____
_____

Notes:
_____
_____

Closing breath cue:

Inhale for 4, hold for 2, exhale for 6 — repeat 3 times.

| JAN | FEB | MAR | APR | MAY | JUN | JUL | AUG | SEP | OCT | NOV | DEC |

1 2 3 4 5 6 7 8 9 10 11 12 13 14 15 16 17 18 19 20 21 22 23 24 25 26 27 28 29 30 31

Daily Morning Reset

(For mental clarity + emotional grounding)

Today, my body feels...

- ☐ Tense
- ☐ Rested
- ☐ Scattered
- ☐ Heavy
- ☐ Neutral
- ☐ Something else: _____

One thing weighing on me today is...

_____
_____
_____
_____
_____

Emotion I'm carrying into today:

_____
_____
_____
_____
_____

What I need emotionally right now:

☐ Space
☐ Encouragement
☐ Boundaries
☐ Rest
☐ Focus
☐ Connection
☐ Other: _____

My intention for today:
A sentence or two that feels doable, gentle, and honest.

_____
_____
_____

A micro-practice to begin the day:
(Choose one)

- 1-minute grounding breath

- Soften your jaw + drop your shoulders

- Step outside for 3 deep breaths

- Name three things supporting you today

Daily Evening Reflection Pages
(For emotional processing + nervous system unwinding)

Where did stress show up today?

Body: _____
Mind: _____
Emotions: _____

How did I respond?

☐ Reacted quickly
☐ Shut down
☐ Over-functioned
☐ Avoided
☐ Paused
☐ Responded intentionally

Notes:
_____
_____
_____

What part of me needed more care?

_____
_____
_____

A moment I'm proud of today:
_____
_____
_____
_____
_____

Something I want to release tonight:
_____
_____
_____
_____
_____

Notes:
_____
_____
_____

Closing breath cue:

Inhale for 4, hold for 2, exhale for 6 — repeat 3 times.

JAN FEB MAR APR MAY JUN JUL AUG SEP OCT NOV DEC
1 2 3 4 5 6 7 8 9 10 11 12 13 14 15 16 17 18 19 20 21 22 23 24 25 26 27 28 29 30 31

Daily Morning Reset

(For mental clarity + emotional grounding)

Today, my body feels…

☐ Tense
☐ Rested
☐ Scattered
☐ Heavy
☐ Neutral
☐ Something else: _____

One thing weighing on me today is…

_____
_____
_____
_____
_____

Emotion I'm carrying into today:

_____
_____
_____
_____
_____

What I need emotionally right now:

☐ Space
☐ Encouragement
☐ Boundaries
☐ Rest
☐ Focus
☐ Connection
☐ Other: _____

My intention for today:
A sentence or two that feels doable, gentle, and honest.

_____
_____
_____

A micro-practice to begin the day:
(Choose one)

- 1-minute grounding breath

- Soften your jaw + drop your shoulders

- Step outside for 3 deep breaths

- Name three things supporting you today

Daily Evening Reflection Pages
(For emotional processing + nervous system unwinding)

Where did stress show up today?

Body: _____
Mind: _____
Emotions: _____

How did I respond?
- ☐ Reacted quickly
- ☐ Shut down
- ☐ Over-functioned
- ☐ Avoided
- ☐ Paused
- ☐ Responded intentionally

Notes:
_____
_____
_____

What part of me needed more care?
_____
_____
_____

A moment I'm proud of today:

_____
_____
_____
_____
_____

Something I want to release tonight:

_____
_____
_____
_____
_____

Notes:

_____
_____
_____

Closing breath cue:

Inhale for 4, hold for 2, exhale for 6 — repeat 3 times.

JAN	FEB	MAR	APR	MAY	JUN	JUL	AUG	SEP	OCT	NOV	DEC

1 2 3 4 5 6 7 8 9 10 11 12 13 14 15 16 17 18 19 20 21 22 23 24 25 26 27 28 29 30 31

Daily Morning Reset
(For mental clarity + emotional grounding)

Today, my body feels…

- ☐ Tense
- ☐ Rested
- ☐ Scattered
- ☐ Heavy
- ☐ Neutral
- ☐ Something else: _____

One thing weighing on me today is…

_____
_____
_____
_____
_____

Emotion I'm carrying into today:

_____
_____
_____
_____

What I need emotionally right now:

☐ Space
☐ Encouragement
☐ Boundaries
☐ Rest
☐ Focus
☐ Connection
☐ Other: _____

My intention for today:

A sentence or two that feels doable, gentle, and honest.

_____
_____
_____

A micro-practice to begin the day:
(Choose one)

- 1-minute grounding breath

- Soften your jaw + drop your shoulders

- Step outside for 3 deep breaths

- Name three things supporting you today

Daily Evening Reflection Pages
(For emotional processing + nervous system unwinding)

Where did stress show up today?

Body: _____
Mind: _____
Emotions: _____

How did I respond?

☐ Reacted quickly
☐ Shut down
☐ Over-functioned
☐ Avoided
☐ Paused
☐ Responded intentionally

Notes:
_____
_____
_____

What part of me needed more care?

_____
_____
_____
_____

A moment I'm proud of today:
_____
_____
_____
_____
_____

Something I want to release tonight:
_____
_____
_____
_____
_____

Notes:
_____
_____
_____

Closing breath cue:

Inhale for 4, hold for 2, exhale for 6 — repeat 3 times.

JAN	FEB	MAR	APR	MAY	JUN	JUL	AUG	SEP	OCT	NOV	DEC

1 2 3 4 5 6 7 8 9 10 11 12 13 14 15 16 17 18 19 20 21 22 23 24 25 26 27 28 29 30 31

Daily Morning Reset
(For mental clarity + emotional grounding)

Today, my body feels...

☐ Tense
☐ Rested
☐ Scattered
☐ Heavy
☐ Neutral
☐ Something else: _____

One thing weighing on me today is...

_____
_____
_____
_____
_____

Emotion I'm carrying into today:

_____
_____
_____
_____
_____

What I need emotionally right now:

- ☐ Space
- ☐ Encouragement
- ☐ Boundaries
- ☐ Rest
- ☐ Focus
- ☐ Connection
- ☐ Other: _____

My intention for today:
A sentence or two that feels doable, gentle, and honest.

_____
_____
_____

A micro-practice to begin the day:
(Choose one)

- 1-minute grounding breath

- Soften your jaw + drop your shoulders

- Step outside for 3 deep breaths

- Name three things supporting you today

Daily Evening Reflection Pages
(For emotional processing + nervous system unwinding)

Where did stress show up today?

Body: _____
Mind: _____
Emotions: _____

How did I respond?

- ☐ Reacted quickly
- ☐ Shut down
- ☐ Over-functioned
- ☐ Avoided
- ☐ Paused
- ☐ Responded intentionally

Notes:
_____
_____
_____

What part of me needed more care?

_____
_____
_____
_____

A moment I'm proud of today:
_____
_____
_____
_____
_____
_____

Something I want to release tonight:
_____
_____
_____
_____
_____
_____

Notes:
_____
_____
_____

Closing breath cue:
Inhale for 4, hold for 2, exhale for 6 — repeat 3 times.

Weekly Reflection

Energy Check-In

What drained me this week?

_____
_____
_____

What restored me this week?

_____
_____
_____

Emotional Patterns I Noticed

- When did I override myself?

- When did I honor my capacity?

- What emotion repeated most?

Notes:
_____
_____

A boundary I need for next week:
_____
_____

One small shift that would support me next week:
_____
_____

Weekly Stress Pattern Awareness Worksheet

What My Stress Cycle This Week Looked Like:

Trigger → Reaction → Emotion → Behavior → Aftermath

Trigger: _____   Trigger: _____   Trigger: _____
Reaction: _____   Reaction: _____   Reaction: _____
Emotion: _____   Emotion: _____   Emotion: _____
Behavior: _____   Behavior: _____   Behavior: _____
Aftermath: _____ Aftermath: _____ Aftermath: _____

What my body did under stress:

- ☐ Tight chest
- ☐ Stomach tension
- ☐ Shallow breathing
- ☐ Head pressure
- ☐ Frozen / shut down
- ☐ Other: _____

What I needed in those moments:

- ☐ Slowness
- ☐ Clarity
- ☐ Space
- ☐ Reassurance
- ☐ Regulation
- ☐ Boundaries

Notes:

_____

_____

JAN	FEB	MAR	APR	MAY	JUN	JUL	AUG	SEP	OCT	NOV	DEC

1 2 3 4 5 6 7 8 9 10 11 12 13 14 15 16 17 18 19 20 21 22 23 24 25 26 27 28 29 30 31

Daily Morning Reset
(For mental clarity + emotional grounding)

Today, my body feels...

☐ Tense
☐ Rested
☐ Scattered
☐ Heavy
☐ Neutral
☐ Something else: _____

One thing weighing on me today is...

_____
_____
_____
_____
_____

Emotion I'm carrying into today:

_____
_____
_____
_____
_____

What I need emotionally right now:

- ☐ Space
- ☐ Encouragement
- ☐ Boundaries
- ☐ Rest
- ☐ Focus
- ☐ Connection
- ☐ Other: _____

My intention for today:

A sentence or two that feels doable, gentle, and honest.

_____
_____
_____

A micro-practice to begin the day:
(Choose one)

- 1-minute grounding breath

- Soften your jaw + drop your shoulders

- Step outside for 3 deep breaths

- Name three things supporting you today

Daily Evening Reflection Pages
(For emotional processing + nervous system unwinding)

Where did stress show up today?

Body: _____
Mind: _____
Emotions: _____

How did I respond?

☐ Reacted quickly
☐ Shut down
☐ Over-functioned
☐ Avoided
☐ Paused
☐ Responded intentionally

Notes:
_____
_____
_____

What part of me needed more care?
_____
_____
_____

A moment I'm proud of today:
_____
_____
_____
_____
_____

Something I want to release tonight:
_____
_____
_____
_____
_____
_____

Notes:
_____
_____
_____

Closing breath cue:

Inhale for 4, hold for 2, exhale for 6 — repeat 3 times.

JAN   FEB   MAR   APR   MAY   JUN   JUL   AUG   SEP   OCT   NOV   DEC
1 2 3 4 5 6 7 8 9 10 11 12 13 14 15 16 17 18 19 20 21 22 23 24 25 26 27 28 29 30 31

Daily Morning Reset
(For mental clarity + emotional grounding)

Today, my body feels...

☐ Tense
☐ Rested
☐ Scattered
☐ Heavy
☐ Neutral
☐ Something else: _____

One thing weighing on me today is...

_____
_____
_____
_____
_____

Emotion I'm carrying into today:

_____
_____
_____
_____
_____

What I need emotionally right now:

☐ Space
☐ Encouragement
☐ Boundaries
☐ Rest
☐ Focus
☐ Connection
☐ Other: _____

My intention for today:
A sentence or two that feels doable, gentle, and honest.

_____
_____
_____

A micro-practice to begin the day:
(Choose one)

- 1-minute grounding breath

- Soften your jaw + drop your shoulders

- Step outside for 3 deep breaths

- Name three things supporting you today

Daily Evening Reflection Pages
(For emotional processing + nervous system unwinding)

Where did stress show up today?

Body: _____
Mind: _____
Emotions: _____

How did I respond?

☐ Reacted quickly
☐ Shut down
☐ Over-functioned
☐ Avoided
☐ Paused
☐ Responded intentionally

Notes:
_____
_____
_____

What part of me needed more care?

_____
_____
_____
_____

A moment I'm proud of today:

_____
_____
_____
_____
_____

Something I want to release tonight:

_____
_____
_____
_____
_____

Notes:

_____
_____
_____

Closing breath cue:

Inhale for 4, hold for 2, exhale for 6 — repeat 3 times.

JAN　　FEB　　MAR　　APR　　MAY　　JUN　　JUL　　AUG　　SEP　　OCT　　NOV　　DEC
1 2 3 4 5 6 7 8 9 10 11 12 13 14 15 16 17 18 19 20 21 22 23 24 25 26 27 28 29 30 31

Daily Morning Reset
(For mental clarity + emotional grounding)

Today, my body feels…

- ☐ Tense
- ☐ Rested
- ☐ Scattered
- ☐ Heavy
- ☐ Neutral
- ☐ Something else: _____

One thing weighing on me today is…

_____
_____
_____
_____

Emotion I'm carrying into today:

_____
_____
_____
_____

What I need emotionally right now:

☐ Space
☐ Encouragement
☐ Boundaries
☐ Rest
☐ Focus
☐ Connection
☐ Other: _____

My intention for today:
A sentence or two that feels doable, gentle, and honest.

_____
_____
_____

A micro-practice to begin the day:
(Choose one)

- 1-minute grounding breath

- Soften your jaw + drop your shoulders

- Step outside for 3 deep breaths

- Name three things supporting you today

Daily Evening Reflection Pages
(For emotional processing + nervous system unwinding)

Where did stress show up today?

Body: _____
Mind: _____
Emotions: _____

How did I respond?

- ☐ Reacted quickly
- ☐ Shut down
- ☐ Over-functioned
- ☐ Avoided
- ☐ Paused
- ☐ Responded intentionally

Notes:
_____
_____
_____

What part of me needed more care?

_____
_____
_____

A moment I'm proud of today:
_____
_____
_____
_____
_____

Something I want to release tonight:
_____
_____
_____
_____
_____
_____

Notes:
_____
_____
_____

Closing breath cue:

Inhale for 4, hold for 2, exhale for 6 — repeat 3 times.

| JAN | FEB | MAR | APR | MAY | JUN | JUL | AUG | SEP | OCT | NOV | DEC |

1 2 3 4 5 6 7 8 9 10 11 12 13 14 15 16 17 18 19 20 21 22 23 24 25 26 27 28 29 30 31

Daily Morning Reset
(For mental clarity + emotional grounding)

Today, my body feels…

☐ Tense
☐ Rested
☐ Scattered
☐ Heavy
☐ Neutral
☐ Something else: _____

One thing weighing on me today is…

_____
_____
_____
_____
_____

Emotion I'm carrying into today:

_____
_____
_____
_____
_____

What I need emotionally right now:

☐ Space
☐ Encouragement
☐ Boundaries
☐ Rest
☐ Focus
☐ Connection
☐ Other: _____

My intention for today:

A sentence or two that feels doable, gentle, and honest.

_____
_____
_____

A micro-practice to begin the day:
(Choose one)

- 1-minute grounding breath

- Soften your jaw + drop your shoulders

- Step outside for 3 deep breaths

- Name three things supporting you today

Daily Evening Reflection Pages
(For emotional processing + nervous system unwinding)

Where did stress show up today?

Body: _____
Mind: _____
Emotions: _____

How did I respond?

☐ Reacted quickly
☐ Shut down
☐ Over-functioned
☐ Avoided
☐ Paused
☐ Responded intentionally

Notes:
_____
_____
_____

What part of me needed more care?

_____
_____
_____

A moment I'm proud of today:
_____
_____
_____
_____
_____

Something I want to release tonight:
_____
_____
_____
_____
_____

Notes:
_____
_____

Closing breath cue:

Inhale for 4, hold for 2, exhale for 6 — repeat 3 times.

JAN	FEB	MAR	APR	MAY	JUN	JUL	AUG	SEP	OCT	NOV	DEC

1 2 3 4 5 6 7 8 9 10 11 12 13 14 15 16 17 18 19 20 21 22 23 24 25 26 27 28 29 30 31

Daily Morning Reset
(For mental clarity + emotional grounding)

Today, my body feels...

☐ Tense
☐ Rested
☐ Scattered
☐ Heavy
☐ Neutral
☐ Something else: _____

One thing weighing on me today is...

_____
_____
_____
_____
_____

Emotion I'm carrying into today:

_____
_____
_____
_____
_____

What I need emotionally right now:

☐ Space
☐ Encouragement
☐ Boundaries
☐ Rest
☐ Focus
☐ Connection
☐ Other: _____

My intention for today:
A sentence or two that feels doable, gentle, and honest.

_____
_____
_____

A micro-practice to begin the day:
(Choose one)

- 1-minute grounding breath

- Soften your jaw + drop your shoulders

- Step outside for 3 deep breaths

- Name three things supporting you today

Daily Evening Reflection Pages
(For emotional processing + nervous system unwinding)

Where did stress show up today?

Body: _____
Mind: _____
Emotions: _____

How did I respond?
- ☐ Reacted quickly
- ☐ Shut down
- ☐ Over-functioned
- ☐ Avoided
- ☐ Paused
- ☐ Responded intentionally

Notes:
_____
_____
_____

What part of me needed more care?
_____
_____
_____
_____

A moment I'm proud of today:
_____
_____
_____
_____
_____

Something I want to release tonight:
_____
_____
_____
_____
_____

Notes:
_____
_____

Closing breath cue:

Inhale for 4, hold for 2, exhale for 6 — repeat 3 times.

JAN FEB MAR APR MAY JUN JUL AUG SEP OCT NOV DEC
1 2 3 4 5 6 7 8 9 10 11 12 13 14 15 16 17 18 19 20 21 22 23 24 25 26 27 28 29 30 31

Daily Morning Reset
(For mental clarity + emotional grounding)

Today, my body feels...

☐ Tense
☐ Rested
☐ Scattered
☐ Heavy
☐ Neutral
☐ Something else: _____

One thing weighing on me today is...

_____
_____
_____
_____
_____

Emotion I'm carrying into today:

_____
_____
_____
_____

What I need emotionally right now:

☐ Space
☐ Encouragement
☐ Boundaries
☐ Rest
☐ Focus
☐ Connection
☐ Other: _____

My intention for today:
A sentence or two that feels doable, gentle, and honest.

_____
_____
_____

A micro-practice to begin the day:
(Choose one)

- 1-minute grounding breath

- Soften your jaw + drop your shoulders

- Step outside for 3 deep breaths

- Name three things supporting you today

Daily Evening Reflection Pages
(For emotional processing + nervous system unwinding)

Where did stress show up today?

Body: _____
Mind: _____
Emotions: _____

How did I respond?

☐ Reacted quickly
☐ Shut down
☐ Over-functioned
☐ Avoided
☐ Paused
☐ Responded intentionally

Notes:
_____
_____
_____

What part of me needed more care?

_____
_____
_____
_____

A moment I'm proud of today:

_____
_____
_____
_____
_____

Something I want to release tonight:

_____
_____
_____
_____
_____

Notes:

_____
_____

Closing breath cue:

Inhale for 4, hold for 2, exhale for 6 — repeat 3 times.

JAN	FEB	MAR	APR	MAY	JUN	JUL	AUG	SEP	OCT	NOV	DEC

1 2 3 4 5 6 7 8 9 10 11 12 13 14 15 16 17 18 19 20 21 22 23 24 25 26 27 28 29 30 31

Daily Morning Reset
(For mental clarity + emotional grounding)

Today, my body feels…

☐ Tense
☐ Rested
☐ Scattered
☐ Heavy
☐ Neutral
☐ Something else: _____

One thing weighing on me today is…

_____
_____
_____
_____
_____

Emotion I'm carrying into today:

_____
_____
_____
_____
_____

What I need emotionally right now:

☐ Space
☐ Encouragement
☐ Boundaries
☐ Rest
☐ Focus
☐ Connection
☐ Other: _____

My intention for today:
A sentence or two that feels doable, gentle, and honest.

_____
_____
_____

A micro-practice to begin the day:
(Choose one)

- 1-minute grounding breath

- Soften your jaw + drop your shoulders

- Step outside for 3 deep breaths

- Name three things supporting you today

Daily Evening Reflection Pages
(For emotional processing + nervous system unwinding)

Where did stress show up today?

Body: _____
Mind: _____
Emotions: _____

How did I respond?

☐ Reacted quickly
☐ Shut down
☐ Over-functioned
☐ Avoided
☐ Paused
☐ Responded intentionally

Notes:
_____
_____
_____

What part of me needed more care?
_____
_____
_____
_____

A moment I'm proud of today:
_____
_____
_____
_____
_____

Something I want to release tonight:
_____
_____
_____
_____
_____

Notes:
_____
_____
_____

Closing breath cue:

Inhale for 4, hold for 2, exhale for 6 — repeat 3 times.

Weekly Reflection

Energy Check-In

What drained me this week?

_____
_____
_____

What restored me this week?

_____
_____
_____

Emotional Patterns I Noticed

- When did I override myself?

- When did I honor my capacity?

- What emotion repeated most?

Notes:
_____
_____

A boundary I need for next week:
_____
_____

One small shift that would support me next week:
_____
_____

Weekly Stress Pattern Awareness Worksheet

What My Stress Cycle This Week Looked Like:

Trigger → Reaction → Emotion → Behavior → Aftermath

Trigger: _____ Trigger: _____ Trigger: _____
Reaction: _____ Reaction: _____ Reaction: _____
Emotion: _____ Emotion: _____ Emotion: _____
Behavior: _____ Behavior: _____ Behavior: _____
Aftermath: _____ Aftermath: _____ Aftermath: _____

What my body did under stress:

- ☐ Tight chest
- ☐ Stomach tension
- ☐ Shallow breathing
- ☐ Head pressure
- ☐ Frozen / shut down
- ☐ Other: _____

What I needed in those moments:

- ☐ Slowness
- ☐ Clarity
- ☐ Space
- ☐ Reassurance
- ☐ Regulation
- ☐ Boundaries

Notes:

_____

_____

JAN FEB MAR APR MAY JUN JUL AUG SEP OCT NOV DEC
1 2 3 4 5 6 7 8 9 10 11 12 13 14 15 16 17 18 19 20 21 22 23 24 25 26 27 28 29 30 31

Daily Morning Reset

(For mental clarity + emotional grounding)

Today, my body feels...

☐ Tense
☐ Rested
☐ Scattered
☐ Heavy
☐ Neutral
☐ Something else: _____

One thing weighing on me today is...

_____
_____
_____
_____
_____

Emotion I'm carrying into today:

_____
_____
_____
_____
_____

What I need emotionally right now:

☐ Space
☐ Encouragement
☐ Boundaries
☐ Rest
☐ Focus
☐ Connection
☐ Other: _____

My intention for today:

A sentence or two that feels doable, gentle, and honest.

_____
_____
_____

A micro-practice to begin the day:
(Choose one)

- 1-minute grounding breath

- Soften your jaw + drop your shoulders

- Step outside for 3 deep breaths

- Name three things supporting you today

Daily Evening Reflection Pages
(For emotional processing + nervous system unwinding)

Where did stress show up today?

Body: _____
Mind: _____
Emotions: _____

How did I respond?

- ☐ Reacted quickly
- ☐ Shut down
- ☐ Over-functioned
- ☐ Avoided
- ☐ Paused
- ☐ Responded intentionally

Notes:
_____
_____
_____

What part of me needed more care?

_____
_____
_____
_____

A moment I'm proud of today:
_____
_____
_____
_____
_____

Something I want to release tonight:
_____
_____
_____
_____
_____

Notes:
_____
_____
_____

Closing breath cue:

Inhale for 4, hold for 2, exhale for 6 — repeat 3 times.

| JAN | FEB | MAR | APR | MAY | JUN | JUL | AUG | SEP | OCT | NOV | DEC |

1 2 3 4 5 6 7 8 9 10 11 12 13 14 15 16 17 18 19 20 21 22 23 24 25 26 27 28 29 30 31

Daily Morning Reset

(For mental clarity + emotional grounding)

Today, my body feels…

☐ Tense
☐ Rested
☐ Scattered
☐ Heavy
☐ Neutral
☐ Something else: _____

One thing weighing on me today is…

_____
_____
_____
_____
_____

Emotion I'm carrying into today:

_____
_____
_____
_____
_____

What I need emotionally right now:

☐ Space
☐ Encouragement
☐ Boundaries
☐ Rest
☐ Focus
☐ Connection
☐ Other: _____

My intention for today:
A sentence or two that feels doable, gentle, and honest.

_____
_____
_____

A micro-practice to begin the day:
(Choose one)

- 1-minute grounding breath

- Soften your jaw + drop your shoulders

- Step outside for 3 deep breaths

- Name three things supporting you today

Daily Evening Reflection Pages
(For emotional processing + nervous system unwinding)

Where did stress show up today?

Body: _____
Mind: _____
Emotions: _____

How did I respond?

- ☐ Reacted quickly
- ☐ Shut down
- ☐ Over-functioned
- ☐ Avoided
- ☐ Paused
- ☐ Responded intentionally

Notes:
_____
_____
_____

What part of me needed more care?
_____
_____
_____
_____

A moment I'm proud of today:

_____
_____
_____
_____
_____

Something I want to release tonight:

_____
_____
_____
_____
_____

Notes:

_____
_____

Closing breath cue:

Inhale for 4, hold for 2, exhale for 6 — repeat 3 times.

JAN	FEB	MAR	APR	MAY	JUN	JUL	AUG	SEP	OCT	NOV	DEC

1 2 3 4 5 6 7 8 9 10 11 12 13 14 15 16 17 18 19 20 21 22 23 24 25 26 27 28 29 30 31

Daily Morning Reset
(For mental clarity + emotional grounding)

Today, my body feels...

☐ Tense
☐ Rested
☐ Scattered
☐ Heavy
☐ Neutral
☐ Something else: _____

One thing weighing on me today is...

_____
_____
_____
_____
_____

Emotion I'm carrying into today:

_____
_____
_____
_____
_____

What I need emotionally right now:

☐ Space
☐ Encouragement
☐ Boundaries
☐ Rest
☐ Focus
☐ Connection
☐ Other: _____

My intention for today:
A sentence or two that feels doable, gentle, and honest.

_____
_____
_____

A micro-practice to begin the day:
(Choose one)

- 1-minute grounding breath

- Soften your jaw + drop your shoulders

- Step outside for 3 deep breaths

- Name three things supporting you today

Daily Evening Reflection Pages
(For emotional processing + nervous system unwinding)

Where did stress show up today?

Body: _____
Mind: _____
Emotions: _____

How did I respond?

☐ Reacted quickly
☐ Shut down
☐ Over-functioned
☐ Avoided
☐ Paused
☐ Responded intentionally

Notes:
_____
_____
_____

What part of me needed more care?

_____
_____
_____
_____

A moment I'm proud of today:
_____
_____
_____
_____
_____

Something I want to release tonight:
_____
_____
_____
_____
_____

Notes:
_____
_____
_____

Closing breath cue:

Inhale for 4, hold for 2, exhale for 6 — repeat 3 times.

JAN FEB MAR APR MAY JUN JUL AUG SEP OCT NOV DEC
1 2 3 4 5 6 7 8 9 10 11 12 13 14 15 16 17 18 19 20 21 22 23 24 25 26 27 28 29 30 31

Daily Morning Reset

(For mental clarity + emotional grounding)

Today, my body feels...

☐ Tense
☐ Rested
☐ Scattered
☐ Heavy
☐ Neutral
☐ Something else: _____

One thing weighing on me today is...

_____
_____
_____
_____
_____

Emotion I'm carrying into today:

_____
_____
_____
_____
_____

What I need emotionally right now:

☐ Space
☐ Encouragement
☐ Boundaries
☐ Rest
☐ Focus
☐ Connection
☐ Other: _____

My intention for today:
A sentence or two that feels doable, gentle, and honest.

_____
_____
_____

A micro-practice to begin the day:
(Choose one)

- 1-minute grounding breath

- Soften your jaw + drop your shoulders

- Step outside for 3 deep breaths

- Name three things supporting you today

Daily Evening Reflection Pages
(For emotional processing + nervous system unwinding)

Where did stress show up today?

Body: _____
Mind: _____
Emotions: _____

How did I respond?

☐ Reacted quickly
☐ Shut down
☐ Over-functioned
☐ Avoided
☐ Paused
☐ Responded intentionally

Notes:
_____
_____
_____

What part of me needed more care?

_____
_____
_____

A moment I'm proud of today:
_____
_____
_____
_____
_____

Something I want to release tonight:
_____
_____
_____
_____
_____
_____

Notes:
_____
_____
_____

Closing breath cue:

Inhale for 4, hold for 2, exhale for 6 — repeat 3 times.

JAN	FEB	MAR	APR	MAY	JUN	JUL	AUG	SEP	OCT	NOV	DEC

1 2 3 4 5 6 7 8 9 10 11 12 13 14 15 16 17 18 19 20 21 22 23 24 25 26 27 28 29 30 31

Daily Morning Reset

(For mental clarity + emotional grounding)

Today, my body feels...

☐ Tense
☐ Rested
☐ Scattered
☐ Heavy
☐ Neutral
☐ Something else: _____

One thing weighing on me today is...

_____
_____
_____
_____
_____

Emotion I'm carrying into today:

_____
_____
_____
_____
_____

What I need emotionally right now:

☐ Space
☐ Encouragement
☐ Boundaries
☐ Rest
☐ Focus
☐ Connection
☐ Other: _____

My intention for today:

A sentence or two that feels doable, gentle, and honest.

_____
_____
_____

A micro-practice to begin the day:
(Choose one)

- 1-minute grounding breath

- Soften your jaw + drop your shoulders

- Step outside for 3 deep breaths

- Name three things supporting you today

Daily Evening Reflection Pages
(For emotional processing + nervous system unwinding)

Where did stress show up today?

Body: _____
Mind: _____
Emotions: _____

How did I respond?

☐ Reacted quickly
☐ Shut down
☐ Over-functioned
☐ Avoided
☐ Paused
☐ Responded intentionally

Notes:
_____
_____
_____

What part of me needed more care?

_____
_____
_____
_____

A moment I'm proud of today:
_____
_____
_____
_____
_____

Something I want to release tonight:
_____
_____
_____
_____
_____

Notes:
_____
_____
_____

Closing breath cue:
Inhale for 4, hold for 2, exhale for 6 — repeat 3 times.

JAN   FEB   MAR   APR   MAY   JUN   JUL   AUG   SEP   OCT   NOV   DEC
1 2 3 4 5 6 7 8 9 10 11 12 13 14 15 16 17 18 19 20 21 22 23 24 25 26 27 28 29 30 31

Daily Morning Reset
(For mental clarity + emotional grounding)

Today, my body feels...

☐ Tense
☐ Rested
☐ Scattered
☐ Heavy
☐ Neutral
☐ Something else: _____

One thing weighing on me today is...

_____
_____
_____
_____
_____

Emotion I'm carrying into today:

_____
_____
_____
_____
_____

What I need emotionally right now:

☐ Space
☐ Encouragement
☐ Boundaries
☐ Rest
☐ Focus
☐ Connection
☐ Other: _____

My intention for today:

A sentence or two that feels doable, gentle, and honest.

_____
_____
_____

A micro-practice to begin the day:
(Choose one)

- 1-minute grounding breath

- Soften your jaw + drop your shoulders

- Step outside for 3 deep breaths

- Name three things supporting you today

Daily Evening Reflection Pages
(For emotional processing + nervous system unwinding)

Where did stress show up today?

Body: _____
Mind: _____
Emotions: _____

How did I respond?

- ☐ Reacted quickly
- ☐ Shut down
- ☐ Over-functioned
- ☐ Avoided
- ☐ Paused
- ☐ Responded intentionally

Notes:
_____
_____
_____

What part of me needed more care?

_____
_____
_____
_____

A moment I'm proud of today:
_____
_____
_____
_____
_____
_____

Something I want to release tonight:
_____
_____
_____
_____
_____
_____

Notes:
_____
_____
_____

Closing breath cue:
Inhale for 4, hold for 2, exhale for 6 — repeat 3 times.

JAN   FEB   MAR   APR   MAY   JUN   JUL   AUG   SEP   OCT   NOV   DEC
1 2 3 4 5 6 7 8 9 10 11 12 13 14 15 16 17 18 19 20 21 22 23 24 25 26 27 28 29 30 31

Daily Morning Reset

(For mental clarity + emotional grounding)

Today, my body feels...

☐ Tense
☐ Rested
☐ Scattered
☐ Heavy
☐ Neutral
☐ Something else: _____

One thing weighing on me today is...

_____
_____
_____
_____
_____

Emotion I'm carrying into today:

_____
_____
_____
_____
_____

What I need emotionally right now:

☐ Space
☐ Encouragement
☐ Boundaries
☐ Rest
☐ Focus
☐ Connection
☐ Other: _____

My intention for today:
A sentence or two that feels doable, gentle, and honest.

_____
_____
_____

A micro-practice to begin the day:
(Choose one)

- 1-minute grounding breath

- Soften your jaw + drop your shoulders

- Step outside for 3 deep breaths

- Name three things supporting you today

Daily Evening Reflection Pages
(For emotional processing + nervous system unwinding)

Where did stress show up today?

Body: _____
Mind: _____
Emotions: _____

How did I respond?

☐ Reacted quickly
☐ Shut down
☐ Over-functioned
☐ Avoided
☐ Paused
☐ Responded intentionally

Notes:
_____
_____
_____

What part of me needed more care?

_____
_____
_____
_____

A moment I'm proud of today:
_____
_____
_____
_____
_____

Something I want to release tonight:
_____
_____
_____
_____
_____

Notes:
_____
_____

Closing breath cue:

Inhale for 4, hold for 2, exhale for 6 — repeat 3 times.

Weekly Reflection

Energy Check-In

What drained me this week?

_____
_____
_____

What restored me this week?

_____
_____
_____

Emotional Patterns I Noticed

- When did I override myself?

- When did I honor my capacity?

- What emotion repeated most?

Notes:
_____
_____

A boundary I need for next week:
_____
_____

One small shift that would support me next week:
_____
_____

Weekly Stress Pattern Awareness Worksheet

What My Stress Cycle This Week Looked Like:

Trigger → Reaction → Emotion → Behavior → Aftermath

Trigger: _____   Trigger: _____   Trigger: _____
Reaction: _____   Reaction: _____   Reaction: _____
Emotion: _____   Emotion: _____   Emotion: _____
Behavior: _____   Behavior: _____   Behavior: _____
Aftermath: _____   Aftermath: _____   Aftermath: _____

What my body did under stress:

- ☐ Tight chest
- ☐ Stomach tension
- ☐ Shallow breathing
- ☐ Head pressure
- ☐ Frozen / shut down
- ☐ Other: _____

What I needed in those moments:

- ☐ Slowness
- ☐ Clarity
- ☐ Space
- ☐ Reassurance
- ☐ Regulation
- ☐ Boundaries

Notes:
_____
_____

JAN	FEB	MAR	APR	MAY	JUN	JUL	AUG	SEP	OCT	NOV	DEC

1 2 3 4 5 6 7 8 9 10 11 12 13 14 15 16 17 18 19 20 21 22 23 24 25 26 27 28 29 30 31

Daily Morning Reset
(For mental clarity + emotional grounding)

Today, my body feels...

☐ Tense
☐ Rested
☐ Scattered
☐ Heavy
☐ Neutral
☐ Something else: _____

One thing weighing on me today is...

_____
_____
_____
_____
_____

Emotion I'm carrying into today:

_____
_____
_____
_____
_____

What I need emotionally right now:

☐ Space
☐ Encouragement
☐ Boundaries
☐ Rest
☐ Focus
☐ Connection
☐ Other: _____

My intention for today:
A sentence or two that feels doable, gentle, and honest.

_____
_____
_____

A micro-practice to begin the day:
(Choose one)

- 1-minute grounding breath

- Soften your jaw + drop your shoulders

- Step outside for 3 deep breaths

- Name three things supporting you today

Daily Evening Reflection Pages
(For emotional processing + nervous system unwinding)

Where did stress show up today?

Body: _____
Mind: _____
Emotions: _____

How did I respond?

- ☐ Reacted quickly
- ☐ Shut down
- ☐ Over-functioned
- ☐ Avoided
- ☐ Paused
- ☐ Responded intentionally

Notes:
_____
_____
_____

What part of me needed more care?

_____
_____
_____
_____

A moment I'm proud of today:
_____
_____
_____
_____
_____

Something I want to release tonight:
_____
_____
_____
_____
_____

Notes:
_____
_____

Closing breath cue:

Inhale for 4, hold for 2, exhale for 6 — repeat 3 times.

JAN	FEB	MAR	APR	MAY	JUN	JUL	AUG	SEP	OCT	NOV	DEC

1 2 3 4 5 6 7 8 9 10 11 12 13 14 15 16 17 18 19 20 21 22 23 24 25 26 27 28 29 30 31

Daily Morning Reset
(For mental clarity + emotional grounding)

Today, my body feels…

☐ Tense
☐ Rested
☐ Scattered
☐ Heavy
☐ Neutral
☐ Something else: _____

One thing weighing on me today is…

_____
_____
_____
_____
_____

Emotion I'm carrying into today:

_____
_____
_____
_____
_____

What I need emotionally right now:

☐ Space
☐ Encouragement
☐ Boundaries
☐ Rest
☐ Focus
☐ Connection
☐ Other: _____

My intention for today:

A sentence or two that feels doable, gentle, and honest.

_____
_____
_____

A micro-practice to begin the day:
(Choose one)

- 1-minute grounding breath

- Soften your jaw + drop your shoulders

- Step outside for 3 deep breaths

- Name three things supporting you today

Daily Evening Reflection Pages
(For emotional processing + nervous system unwinding)

Where did stress show up today?

Body: _____
Mind: _____
Emotions: _____

How did I respond?
- ☐ Reacted quickly
- ☐ Shut down
- ☐ Over-functioned
- ☐ Avoided
- ☐ Paused
- ☐ Responded intentionally

Notes:
_____
_____
_____

What part of me needed more care?
_____
_____
_____
_____

A moment I'm proud of today:

_____
_____
_____
_____
_____

Something I want to release tonight:

_____
_____
_____
_____
_____
_____

Notes:

_____
_____
_____

Closing breath cue:

Inhale for 4, hold for 2, exhale for 6 — repeat 3 times.

JAN　　FEB　　MAR　　APR　　MAY　　JUN　　JUL　　AUG　　SEP　　OCT　　NOV　　DEC
1 2 3 4 5 6 7 8 9 10 11 12 13 14 15 16 17 18 19 20 21 22 23 24 25 26 27 28 29 30 31

Daily Morning Reset
(For mental clarity + emotional grounding)

Today, my body feels...

☐ Tense
☐ Rested
☐ Scattered
☐ Heavy
☐ Neutral
☐ Something else: _____

One thing weighing on me today is...

_____
_____
_____
_____
_____

Emotion I'm carrying into today:

_____
_____
_____
_____
_____

What I need emotionally right now:

☐ Space
☐ Encouragement
☐ Boundaries
☐ Rest
☐ Focus
☐ Connection
☐ Other: _____

My intention for today:
A sentence or two that feels doable, gentle, and honest.

_____
_____
_____

A micro-practice to begin the day:
(Choose one)

- 1-minute grounding breath

- Soften your jaw + drop your shoulders

- Step outside for 3 deep breaths

- Name three things supporting you today

Daily Evening Reflection Pages
(For emotional processing + nervous system unwinding)

Where did stress show up today?

Body: _____
Mind: _____
Emotions: _____

How did I respond?

- ☐ Reacted quickly
- ☐ Shut down
- ☐ Over-functioned
- ☐ Avoided
- ☐ Paused
- ☐ Responded intentionally

Notes:
_____
_____
_____

What part of me needed more care?

_____
_____
_____
_____

A moment I'm proud of today:

_____
_____
_____
_____
_____

Something I want to release tonight:

_____
_____
_____
_____
_____

Notes:

_____
_____

Closing breath cue:

Inhale for 4, hold for 2, exhale for 6 — repeat 3 times.

| JAN | FEB | MAR | APR | MAY | JUN | JUL | AUG | SEP | OCT | NOV | DEC |

1 2 3 4 5 6 7 8 9 10 11 12 13 14 15 16 17 18 19 20 21 22 23 24 25 26 27 28 29 30 31

Daily Morning Reset
(For mental clarity + emotional grounding)

Today, my body feels...

☐ Tense
☐ Rested
☐ Scattered
☐ Heavy
☐ Neutral
☐ Something else: _____

One thing weighing on me today is...

_____
_____
_____
_____
_____

Emotion I'm carrying into today:

_____
_____
_____
_____

What I need emotionally right now:

☐ Space
☐ Encouragement
☐ Boundaries
☐ Rest
☐ Focus
☐ Connection
☐ Other: _____

My intention for today:

A sentence or two that feels doable, gentle, and honest.

_____
_____
_____

A micro-practice to begin the day:

(Choose one)

- 1-minute grounding breath

- Soften your jaw + drop your shoulders

- Step outside for 3 deep breaths

- Name three things supporting you today

Daily Evening Reflection Pages
(For emotional processing + nervous system unwinding)

Where did stress show up today?

Body: _____
Mind: _____
Emotions: _____

How did I respond?

- ☐ Reacted quickly
- ☐ Shut down
- ☐ Over-functioned
- ☐ Avoided
- ☐ Paused
- ☐ Responded intentionally

Notes:
_____
_____
_____

What part of me needed more care?
_____
_____
_____
_____

A moment I'm proud of today:
_____
_____
_____
_____
_____

Something I want to release tonight:
_____
_____
_____
_____
_____
_____

Notes:
_____
_____
_____

Closing breath cue:

Inhale for 4, hold for 2, exhale for 6 — repeat 3 times.

JAN	FEB	MAR	APR	MAY	JUN	JUL	AUG	SEP	OCT	NOV	DEC

1 2 3 4 5 6 7 8 9 10 11 12 13 14 15 16 17 18 19 20 21 22 23 24 25 26 27 28 29 30 31

Daily Morning Reset
(For mental clarity + emotional grounding)

Today, my body feels...

☐ Tense
☐ Rested
☐ Scattered
☐ Heavy
☐ Neutral
☐ Something else: _____

One thing weighing on me today is...

_____
_____
_____
_____
_____

Emotion I'm carrying into today:

_____
_____
_____
_____
_____

What I need emotionally right now:

☐ Space
☐ Encouragement
☐ Boundaries
☐ Rest
☐ Focus
☐ Connection
☐ Other: _____

My intention for today:

A sentence or two that feels doable, gentle, and honest.

_____
_____
_____

A micro-practice to begin the day:
(Choose one)

- 1-minute grounding breath

- Soften your jaw + drop your shoulders

- Step outside for 3 deep breaths

- Name three things supporting you today

Daily Evening Reflection Pages
(For emotional processing + nervous system unwinding)

Where did stress show up today?

Body: _____
Mind: _____
Emotions: _____

How did I respond?

☐ Reacted quickly
☐ Shut down
☐ Over-functioned
☐ Avoided
☐ Paused
☐ Responded intentionally

Notes:
_____
_____
_____

What part of me needed more care?
_____
_____
_____
_____

A moment I'm proud of today:
_____
_____
_____
_____
_____

Something I want to release tonight:
_____
_____
_____
_____
_____

Notes:
_____
_____
_____

Closing breath cue:

Inhale for 4, hold for 2, exhale for 6 — repeat 3 times.

JAN	FEB	MAR	APR	MAY	JUN	JUL	AUG	SEP	OCT	NOV	DEC

1 2 3 4 5 6 7 8 9 10 11 12 13 14 15 16 17 18 19 20 21 22 23 24 25 26 27 28 29 30 31

Daily Morning Reset

(For mental clarity + emotional grounding)

Today, my body feels...

☐ Tense
☐ Rested
☐ Scattered
☐ Heavy
☐ Neutral
☐ Something else: _____

One thing weighing on me today is...

_____
_____
_____
_____
_____

Emotion I'm carrying into today:

_____
_____
_____
_____

What I need emotionally right now:

☐ Space
☐ Encouragement
☐ Boundaries
☐ Rest
☐ Focus
☐ Connection
☐ Other: _____

My intention for today:
A sentence or two that feels doable, gentle, and honest.

_____
_____
_____

A micro-practice to begin the day:
(Choose one)

- 1-minute grounding breath

- Soften your jaw + drop your shoulders

- Step outside for 3 deep breaths

- Name three things supporting you today

Daily Evening Reflection Pages
(For emotional processing + nervous system unwinding)

Where did stress show up today?

Body: _____

Mind: _____

Emotions: _____

How did I respond?

- ☐ Reacted quickly
- ☐ Shut down
- ☐ Over-functioned
- ☐ Avoided
- ☐ Paused
- ☐ Responded intentionally

Notes:

_____
_____
_____

What part of me needed more care?

_____
_____
_____
_____

A moment I'm proud of today:
_____
_____
_____
_____
_____

Something I want to release tonight:
_____
_____
_____
_____
_____

Notes:
_____
_____
_____

Closing breath cue:

Inhale for 4, hold for 2, exhale for 6 — repeat 3 times.

JAN	FEB	MAR	APR	MAY	JUN	JUL	AUG	SEP	OCT	NOV	DEC

1 2 3 4 5 6 7 8 9 10 11 12 13 14 15 16 17 18 19 20 21 22 23 24 25 26 27 28 29 30 31

Daily Morning Reset
(For mental clarity + emotional grounding)

Today, my body feels…

☐ Tense
☐ Rested
☐ Scattered
☐ Heavy
☐ Neutral
☐ Something else: _____

One thing weighing on me today is…

_____
_____
_____
_____
_____

Emotion I'm carrying into today:

_____
_____
_____
_____

What I need emotionally right now:

☐ Space
☐ Encouragement
☐ Boundaries
☐ Rest
☐ Focus
☐ Connection
☐ Other: _____

My intention for today:
A sentence or two that feels doable, gentle, and honest.

_____
_____
_____

A micro-practice to begin the day:
(Choose one)

- 1-minute grounding breath

- Soften your jaw + drop your shoulders

- Step outside for 3 deep breaths

- Name three things supporting you today

Daily Evening Reflection Pages
(For emotional processing + nervous system unwinding)

Where did stress show up today?

Body: _____
Mind: _____
Emotions: _____

How did I respond?

☐ Reacted quickly
☐ Shut down
☐ Over-functioned
☐ Avoided
☐ Paused
☐ Responded intentionally

Notes:
_____
_____
_____

What part of me needed more care?
_____
_____
_____

A moment I'm proud of today:
_____
_____
_____
_____
_____

Something I want to release tonight:
_____
_____
_____
_____
_____

Notes:
_____
_____

Closing breath cue:

Inhale for 4, hold for 2, exhale for 6 — repeat 3 times.

Weekly Reflection

Energy Check-In

What drained me this week?

_____
_____
_____

What restored me this week?

_____
_____
_____

Emotional Patterns I Noticed

- When did I override myself?

- When did I honor my capacity?

- What emotion repeated most?

Notes:

_____
_____

A boundary I need for next week:

_____
_____

One small shift that would support me next week:

_____
_____

Weekly Stress Pattern Awareness Worksheet

What My Stress Cycle This Week Looked Like:

Trigger → Reaction → Emotion → Behavior → Aftermath

Trigger: _____ Trigger: _____ Trigger: _____
Reaction: _____ Reaction: _____ Reaction: _____
Emotion: _____ Emotion: _____ Emotion: _____
Behavior: _____ Behavior: _____ Behavior: _____
Aftermath: _____ Aftermath: _____ Aftermath: _____

What my body did under stress:

- ☐ Tight chest
- ☐ Stomach tension
- ☐ Shallow breathing
- ☐ Head pressure
- ☐ Frozen / shut down
- ☐ Other: _____

What I needed in those moments:

- ☐ Slowness
- ☐ Clarity
- ☐ Space
- ☐ Reassurance
- ☐ Regulation
- ☐ Boundaries

Notes:

_____

_____

| JAN | FEB | MAR | APR | MAY | JUN | JUL | AUG | SEP | OCT | NOV | DEC |

1 2 3 4 5 6 7 8 9 10 11 12 13 14 15 16 17 18 19 20 21 22 23 24 25 26 27 28 29 30 31

Daily Morning Reset
(For mental clarity + emotional grounding)

Today, my body feels...

☐ Tense
☐ Rested
☐ Scattered
☐ Heavy
☐ Neutral
☐ Something else: _____

One thing weighing on me today is...

_____
_____
_____
_____
_____

Emotion I'm carrying into today:

_____
_____
_____
_____

What I need emotionally right now:

☐ Space
☐ Encouragement
☐ Boundaries
☐ Rest
☐ Focus
☐ Connection
☐ Other: _____

My intention for today:

A sentence or two that feels doable, gentle, and honest.

_____
_____
_____

A micro-practice to begin the day:
(Choose one)

- 1-minute grounding breath

- Soften your jaw + drop your shoulders

- Step outside for 3 deep breaths

- Name three things supporting you today

Daily Evening Reflection Pages
(For emotional processing + nervous system unwinding)

Where did stress show up today?

Body: _____
Mind: _____
Emotions: _____

How did I respond?

☐ Reacted quickly
☐ Shut down
☐ Over-functioned
☐ Avoided
☐ Paused
☐ Responded intentionally

Notes:
_____
_____
_____

What part of me needed more care?

_____
_____
_____
_____

A moment I'm proud of today:
_____
_____
_____
_____
_____

Something I want to release tonight:
_____
_____
_____
_____
_____
_____

Notes:
_____
_____
_____

Closing breath cue:

Inhale for 4, hold for 2, exhale for 6 — repeat 3 times.

JAN	FEB	MAR	APR	MAY	JUN	JUL	AUG	SEP	OCT	NOV	DEC

1 2 3 4 5 6 7 8 9 10 11 12 13 14 15 16 17 18 19 20 21 22 23 24 25 26 27 28 29 30 31

Daily Morning Reset
(For mental clarity + emotional grounding)

Today, my body feels...

☐ Tense
☐ Rested
☐ Scattered
☐ Heavy
☐ Neutral
☐ Something else: _____

One thing weighing on me today is...

_____
_____
_____
_____

Emotion I'm carrying into today:

_____
_____
_____
_____

What I need emotionally right now:

☐ Space
☐ Encouragement
☐ Boundaries
☐ Rest
☐ Focus
☐ Connection
☐ Other: _____

My intention for today:

A sentence or two that feels doable, gentle, and honest.

_____
_____
_____

A micro-practice to begin the day:
(Choose one)

- 1-minute grounding breath

- Soften your jaw + drop your shoulders

- Step outside for 3 deep breaths

- Name three things supporting you today

Daily Evening Reflection Pages
(For emotional processing + nervous system unwinding)

Where did stress show up today?

Body: _____

Mind: _____

Emotions: _____

How did I respond?

☐ Reacted quickly
☐ Shut down
☐ Over-functioned
☐ Avoided
☐ Paused
☐ Responded intentionally

Notes:
_____
_____
_____

What part of me needed more care?
_____
_____
_____
_____

A moment I'm proud of today:
_____
_____
_____
_____
_____
_____

Something I want to release tonight:
_____
_____
_____
_____
_____
_____

Notes:
_____
_____
_____

Closing breath cue:

Inhale for 4, hold for 2, exhale for 6 — repeat 3 times.

JAN FEB MAR APR MAY JUN JUL AUG SEP OCT NOV DEC
1 2 3 4 5 6 7 8 9 10 11 12 13 14 15 16 17 18 19 20 21 22 23 24 25 26 27 28 29 30 31

Daily Morning Reset
(For mental clarity + emotional grounding)

Today, my body feels…

☐ Tense
☐ Rested
☐ Scattered
☐ Heavy
☐ Neutral
☐ Something else: _____

One thing weighing on me today is…

_____
_____
_____
_____
_____

Emotion I'm carrying into today:

_____
_____
_____
_____

What I need emotionally right now:

☐ Space
☐ Encouragement
☐ Boundaries
☐ Rest
☐ Focus
☐ Connection
☐ Other: _____

My intention for today:

A sentence or two that feels doable, gentle, and honest.

_____
_____
_____

A micro-practice to begin the day:
(Choose one)

- 1-minute grounding breath

- Soften your jaw + drop your shoulders

- Step outside for 3 deep breaths

- Name three things supporting you today

Daily Evening Reflection Pages
(For emotional processing + nervous system unwinding)

Where did stress show up today?

Body: _____
Mind: _____
Emotions: _____

How did I respond?

- ☐ Reacted quickly
- ☐ Shut down
- ☐ Over-functioned
- ☐ Avoided
- ☐ Paused
- ☐ Responded intentionally

Notes:
_____
_____
_____

What part of me needed more care?

_____
_____
_____
_____

A moment I'm proud of today:

_____
_____
_____
_____
_____

Something I want to release tonight:

_____
_____
_____
_____
_____

Notes:

_____
_____
_____

Closing breath cue:

Inhale for 4, hold for 2, exhale for 6 — repeat 3 times.

JAN	FEB	MAR	APR	MAY	JUN	JUL	AUG	SEP	OCT	NOV	DEC

1 2 3 4 5 6 7 8 9 10 11 12 13 14 15 16 17 18 19 20 21 22 23 24 25 26 27 28 29 30 31

Daily Morning Reset
(For mental clarity + emotional grounding)

Today, my body feels…

☐ Tense
☐ Rested
☐ Scattered
☐ Heavy
☐ Neutral
☐ Something else: _____

One thing weighing on me today is…

_____
_____
_____
_____
_____

Emotion I'm carrying into today:

_____
_____
_____
_____
_____

What I need emotionally right now:

☐ Space
☐ Encouragement
☐ Boundaries
☐ Rest
☐ Focus
☐ Connection
☐ Other: _____

My intention for today:
A sentence or two that feels doable, gentle, and honest.

_____
_____
_____

A micro-practice to begin the day:
(Choose one)

- 1-minute grounding breath

- Soften your jaw + drop your shoulders

- Step outside for 3 deep breaths

- Name three things supporting you today

Daily Evening Reflection Pages
(For emotional processing + nervous system unwinding)

Where did stress show up today?

Body: _____
Mind: _____
Emotions: _____

How did I respond?

- ☐ Reacted quickly
- ☐ Shut down
- ☐ Over-functioned
- ☐ Avoided
- ☐ Paused
- ☐ Responded intentionally

Notes:
_____
_____
_____

What part of me needed more care?

_____
_____
_____
_____

A moment I'm proud of today:
_____
_____
_____
_____
_____

Something I want to release tonight:
_____
_____
_____
_____
_____

Notes:
_____
_____
_____

Closing breath cue:

Inhale for 4, hold for 2, exhale for 6 — repeat 3 times.

JAN FEB MAR APR MAY JUN JUL AUG SEP OCT NOV DEC
1 2 3 4 5 6 7 8 9 10 11 12 13 14 15 16 17 18 19 20 21 22 23 24 25 26 27 28 29 30 31

Daily Morning Reset
(For mental clarity + emotional grounding)

Today, my body feels...

☐ Tense
☐ Rested
☐ Scattered
☐ Heavy
☐ Neutral
☐ Something else: _____

One thing weighing on me today is...

_____
_____
_____
_____
_____

Emotion I'm carrying into today:

_____
_____
_____
_____
_____

What I need emotionally right now:

- ☐ Space
- ☐ Encouragement
- ☐ Boundaries
- ☐ Rest
- ☐ Focus
- ☐ Connection
- ☐ Other: _____

My intention for today:

A sentence or two that feels doable, gentle, and honest.

_____
_____
_____

A micro-practice to begin the day:
(Choose one)

- 1-minute grounding breath

- Soften your jaw + drop your shoulders

- Step outside for 3 deep breaths

- Name three things supporting you today

Daily Evening Reflection Pages
(For emotional processing + nervous system unwinding)

Where did stress show up today?

Body: _____

Mind: _____

Emotions: _____

How did I respond?

☐ Reacted quickly
☐ Shut down
☐ Over-functioned
☐ Avoided
☐ Paused
☐ Responded intentionally

Notes:
_____
_____
_____

What part of me needed more care?

_____
_____
_____
_____

A moment I'm proud of today:

_____
_____
_____
_____
_____

Something I want to release tonight:

_____
_____
_____
_____
_____

Notes:

_____
_____
_____

Closing breath cue:

Inhale for 4, hold for 2, exhale for 6 — repeat 3 times.

| JAN | FEB | MAR | APR | MAY | JUN | JUL | AUG | SEP | OCT | NOV | DEC |

1 2 3 4 5 6 7 8 9 10 11 12 13 14 15 16 17 18 19 20 21 22 23 24 25 26 27 28 29 30 31

Daily Morning Reset
(For mental clarity + emotional grounding)

Today, my body feels...

- ☐ Tense
- ☐ Rested
- ☐ Scattered
- ☐ Heavy
- ☐ Neutral
- ☐ Something else: _____

One thing weighing on me today is...

_____
_____
_____
_____
_____

Emotion I'm carrying into today:

_____
_____
_____
_____
_____

What I need emotionally right now:

☐ Space
☐ Encouragement
☐ Boundaries
☐ Rest
☐ Focus
☐ Connection
☐ Other: _____

My intention for today:
A sentence or two that feels doable, gentle, and honest.

_____
_____
_____

A micro-practice to begin the day:
(Choose one)

- 1-minute grounding breath

- Soften your jaw + drop your shoulders

- Step outside for 3 deep breaths

- Name three things supporting you today

Daily Evening Reflection Pages
(For emotional processing + nervous system unwinding)

Where did stress show up today?

Body: _____

Mind: _____

Emotions: _____

How did I respond?

- ☐ Reacted quickly
- ☐ Shut down
- ☐ Over-functioned
- ☐ Avoided
- ☐ Paused
- ☐ Responded intentionally

Notes:
_____
_____
_____

What part of me needed more care?
_____
_____
_____

A moment I'm proud of today:
_____
_____
_____
_____
_____

Something I want to release tonight:
_____
_____
_____
_____
_____

Notes:
_____
_____
_____

Closing breath cue:
Inhale for 4, hold for 2, exhale for 6 — repeat 3 times.

| JAN | FEB | MAR | APR | MAY | JUN | JUL | AUG | SEP | OCT | NOV | DEC |

1 2 3 4 5 6 7 8 9 10 11 12 13 14 15 16 17 18 19 20 21 22 23 24 25 26 27 28 29 30 31

Daily Morning Reset

(For mental clarity + emotional grounding)

Today, my body feels...

☐ Tense
☐ Rested
☐ Scattered
☐ Heavy
☐ Neutral
☐ Something else: _____

One thing weighing on me today is...

_____
_____
_____
_____
_____

Emotion I'm carrying into today:

_____
_____
_____
_____
_____

What I need emotionally right now:

☐ Space
☐ Encouragement
☐ Boundaries
☐ Rest
☐ Focus
☐ Connection
☐ Other: _____

My intention for today:
A sentence or two that feels doable, gentle, and honest.

_____
_____
_____

A micro-practice to begin the day:
(Choose one)

- 1-minute grounding breath

- Soften your jaw + drop your shoulders

- Step outside for 3 deep breaths

- Name three things supporting you today

Daily Evening Reflection Pages
(For emotional processing + nervous system unwinding)

Where did stress show up today?

Body: _____
Mind: _____
Emotions: _____

How did I respond?

☐ Reacted quickly
☐ Shut down
☐ Over-functioned
☐ Avoided
☐ Paused
☐ Responded intentionally

Notes:
_____
_____

What part of me needed more care?

_____
_____
_____

A moment I'm proud of today:
_____
_____
_____
_____
_____
_____

Something I want to release tonight:
_____
_____
_____
_____
_____
_____

Notes:
_____
_____
_____

Closing breath cue:

Inhale for 4, hold for 2, exhale for 6 — repeat 3 times.

Weekly Reflection

Energy Check-In

What drained me this week?

_____
_____
_____

What restored me this week?

_____
_____
_____

Emotional Patterns I Noticed

- When did I override myself?

- When did I honor my capacity?

- What emotion repeated most?

Notes:
_____
_____

A boundary I need for next week:
_____
_____

One small shift that would support me next week:
_____
_____

Weekly Stress Pattern Awareness Worksheet

What My Stress Cycle This Week Looked Like:

Trigger → Reaction → Emotion → Behavior → Aftermath

Trigger: _____
Reaction: _____
Emotion: _____
Behavior: _____
Aftermath: _____

Trigger: _____
Reaction: _____
Emotion: _____
Behavior: _____
Aftermath: _____

Trigger: _____
Reaction: _____
Emotion: _____
Behavior: _____
Aftermath: _____

What my body did under stress:

- ☐ Tight chest
- ☐ Stomach tension
- ☐ Shallow breathing
- ☐ Head pressure
- ☐ Frozen / shut down
- ☐ Other: _____

What I needed in those moments:

- ☐ Slowness
- ☐ Clarity
- ☐ Space
- ☐ Reassurance
- ☐ Regulation
- ☐ Boundaries

Notes:

_____

_____

JAN FEB MAR APR MAY JUN JUL AUG SEP OCT NOV DEC
1 2 3 4 5 6 7 8 9 10 11 12 13 14 15 16 17 18 19 20 21 22 23 24 25 26 27 28 29 30 31

Daily Morning Reset
(For mental clarity + emotional grounding)

Today, my body feels...

☐ Tense
☐ Rested
☐ Scattered
☐ Heavy
☐ Neutral
☐ Something else: _____

One thing weighing on me today is...

_____
_____
_____
_____
_____

Emotion I'm carrying into today:

_____
_____
_____
_____
_____

What I need emotionally right now:

☐ Space
☐ Encouragement
☐ Boundaries
☐ Rest
☐ Focus
☐ Connection
☐ Other: _____

My intention for today:
A sentence or two that feels doable, gentle, and honest.

_____
_____
_____

A micro-practice to begin the day:
(Choose one)

- 1-minute grounding breath

- Soften your jaw + drop your shoulders

- Step outside for 3 deep breaths

- Name three things supporting you today

Daily Evening Reflection Pages
(For emotional processing + nervous system unwinding)

Where did stress show up today?

Body: _____
Mind: _____
Emotions: _____

How did I respond?

☐ Reacted quickly
☐ Shut down
☐ Over-functioned
☐ Avoided
☐ Paused
☐ Responded intentionally

Notes:
_____
_____
_____

What part of me needed more care?

_____
_____
_____
_____

A moment I'm proud of today:
_____
_____
_____
_____
_____

Something I want to release tonight:
_____
_____
_____
_____
_____

Notes:
_____
_____
_____

Closing breath cue:
Inhale for 4, hold for 2, exhale for 6 — repeat 3 times.

JAN	FEB	MAR	APR	MAY	JUN	JUL	AUG	SEP	OCT	NOV	DEC

1 2 3 4 5 6 7 8 9 10 11 12 13 14 15 16 17 18 19 20 21 22 23 24 25 26 27 28 29 30 31

Daily Morning Reset
(For mental clarity + emotional grounding)

Today, my body feels...

☐ Tense
☐ Rested
☐ Scattered
☐ Heavy
☐ Neutral
☐ Something else: _____

One thing weighing on me today is...

_____
_____
_____
_____
_____

Emotion I'm carrying into today:

_____
_____
_____
_____

What I need emotionally right now:

☐ Space
☐ Encouragement
☐ Boundaries
☐ Rest
☐ Focus
☐ Connection
☐ Other: _____

My intention for today:

A sentence or two that feels doable, gentle, and honest.

_____
_____
_____

A micro-practice to begin the day:

(Choose one)

- 1-minute grounding breath

- Soften your jaw + drop your shoulders

- Step outside for 3 deep breaths

- Name three things supporting you today

Daily Evening Reflection Pages
(For emotional processing + nervous system unwinding)

Where did stress show up today?

Body: _____
Mind: _____
Emotions: _____

How did I respond?

☐ Reacted quickly
☐ Shut down
☐ Over-functioned
☐ Avoided
☐ Paused
☐ Responded intentionally

Notes:
_____
_____
_____

What part of me needed more care?
_____
_____
_____

A moment I'm proud of today:

_____
_____
_____
_____
_____
_____

Something I want to release tonight:

_____
_____
_____
_____
_____
_____

Notes:

_____
_____
_____

Closing breath cue:

Inhale for 4, hold for 2, exhale for 6 — repeat 3 times.

JAN FEB MAR APR MAY JUN JUL AUG SEP OCT NOV DEC
1 2 3 4 5 6 7 8 9 10 11 12 13 14 15 16 17 18 19 20 21 22 23 24 25 26 27 28 29 30 31

Daily Morning Reset
(For mental clarity + emotional grounding)

Today, my body feels…

☐ Tense
☐ Rested
☐ Scattered
☐ Heavy
☐ Neutral
☐ Something else: _____

One thing weighing on me today is…

_____
_____
_____
_____
_____

Emotion I'm carrying into today:

_____
_____
_____
_____
_____

What I need emotionally right now:

☐ Space
☐ Encouragement
☐ Boundaries
☐ Rest
☐ Focus
☐ Connection
☐ Other: _____

My intention for today:
A sentence or two that feels doable, gentle, and honest.

_____
_____
_____

A micro-practice to begin the day:
(Choose one)

- 1-minute grounding breath

- Soften your jaw + drop your shoulders

- Step outside for 3 deep breaths

- Name three things supporting you today

Daily Evening Reflection Pages
(For emotional processing + nervous system unwinding)

Where did stress show up today?

Body: _____
Mind: _____
Emotions: _____

How did I respond?

☐ Reacted quickly
☐ Shut down
☐ Over-functioned
☐ Avoided
☐ Paused
☐ Responded intentionally

Notes:
_____
_____
_____

What part of me needed more care?

_____
_____
_____
_____

A moment I'm proud of today:

_____
_____
_____
_____
_____

Something I want to release tonight:

_____
_____
_____
_____
_____

Notes:

_____
_____
_____

Closing breath cue:

Inhale for 4, hold for 2, exhale for 6 — repeat 3 times.

JAN FEB MAR APR MAY JUN JUL AUG SEP OCT NOV DEC
1 2 3 4 5 6 7 8 9 10 11 12 13 14 15 16 17 18 19 20 21 22 23 24 25 26 27 28 29 30 31

Daily Morning Reset

(For mental clarity + emotional grounding)

Today, my body feels...

☐ Tense
☐ Rested
☐ Scattered
☐ Heavy
☐ Neutral
☐ Something else: _____

One thing weighing on me today is...

_____
_____
_____
_____
_____

Emotion I'm carrying into today:

_____
_____
_____
_____
_____

What I need emotionally right now:

- ☐ Space
- ☐ Encouragement
- ☐ Boundaries
- ☐ Rest
- ☐ Focus
- ☐ Connection
- ☐ Other: _____

My intention for today:

A sentence or two that feels doable, gentle, and honest.

_____
_____
_____

A micro-practice to begin the day:

(Choose one)

- 1-minute grounding breath

- Soften your jaw + drop your shoulders

- Step outside for 3 deep breaths

- Name three things supporting you today

Daily Evening Reflection Pages
(For emotional processing + nervous system unwinding)

Where did stress show up today?

Body: _____
Mind: _____
Emotions: _____

How did I respond?

☐ Reacted quickly
☐ Shut down
☐ Over-functioned
☐ Avoided
☐ Paused
☐ Responded intentionally

Notes:
_____
_____
_____

What part of me needed more care?

_____
_____
_____
_____

A moment I'm proud of today:
_____
_____
_____
_____
_____
_____

Something I want to release tonight:
_____
_____
_____
_____
_____
_____

Notes:
_____
_____
_____

Closing breath cue:
Inhale for 4, hold for 2, exhale for 6 — repeat 3 times.

JAN   FEB   MAR   APR   MAY   JUN   JUL   AUG   SEP   OCT   NOV   DEC
1 2 3 4 5 6 7 8 9 10 11 12 13 14 15 16 17 18 19 20 21 22 23 24 25 26 27 28 29 30 31

Daily Morning Reset

(For mental clarity + emotional grounding)

Today, my body feels…

☐ Tense
☐ Rested
☐ Scattered
☐ Heavy
☐ Neutral
☐ Something else: _____

One thing weighing on me today is…

_____
_____
_____
_____
_____

Emotion I'm carrying into today:

_____
_____
_____
_____
_____

What I need emotionally right now:

- ☐ Space
- ☐ Encouragement
- ☐ Boundaries
- ☐ Rest
- ☐ Focus
- ☐ Connection
- ☐ Other: _____

My intention for today:

A sentence or two that feels doable, gentle, and honest.

_____
_____
_____

A micro-practice to begin the day:

(Choose one)

- 1-minute grounding breath

- Soften your jaw + drop your shoulders

- Step outside for 3 deep breaths

- Name three things supporting you today

Daily Evening Reflection Pages
(For emotional processing + nervous system unwinding)

Where did stress show up today?

Body: _____
Mind: _____
Emotions: _____

How did I respond?

- ☐ Reacted quickly
- ☐ Shut down
- ☐ Over-functioned
- ☐ Avoided
- ☐ Paused
- ☐ Responded intentionally

Notes:
_____
_____
_____

What part of me needed more care?

_____
_____
_____
_____

A moment I'm proud of today:
_____
_____
_____
_____
_____

Something I want to release tonight:
_____
_____
_____
_____
_____

Notes:
_____
_____
_____

Closing breath cue:

Inhale for 4, hold for 2, exhale for 6 — repeat 3 times.

JAN FEB MAR APR MAY JUN JUL AUG SEP OCT NOV DEC
1 2 3 4 5 6 7 8 9 10 11 12 13 14 15 16 17 18 19 20 21 22 23 24 25 26 27 28 29 30 31

Daily Morning Reset

(For mental clarity + emotional grounding)

Today, my body feels...

☐ Tense
☐ Rested
☐ Scattered
☐ Heavy
☐ Neutral
☐ Something else: _____

One thing weighing on me today is...

_____
_____
_____
_____
_____

Emotion I'm carrying into today:

_____
_____
_____
_____
_____

What I need emotionally right now:

☐ Space
☐ Encouragement
☐ Boundaries
☐ Rest
☐ Focus
☐ Connection
☐ Other: _____

My intention for today:
A sentence or two that feels doable, gentle, and honest.

_____
_____
_____

A micro-practice to begin the day:
(Choose one)

- 1-minute grounding breath

- Soften your jaw + drop your shoulders

- Step outside for 3 deep breaths

- Name three things supporting you today

Daily Evening Reflection Pages
(For emotional processing + nervous system unwinding)

Where did stress show up today?

Body: _____

Mind: _____

Emotions: _____

How did I respond?

☐ Reacted quickly
☐ Shut down
☐ Over-functioned
☐ Avoided
☐ Paused
☐ Responded intentionally

Notes:

_____
_____
_____

What part of me needed more care?

_____
_____
_____
_____

A moment I'm proud of today:

_____
_____
_____
_____
_____
_____

Something I want to release tonight:

_____
_____
_____
_____
_____
_____

Notes:

_____
_____
_____

Closing breath cue:

Inhale for 4, hold for 2, exhale for 6 — repeat 3 times.

| JAN | FEB | MAR | APR | MAY | JUN | JUL | AUG | SEP | OCT | NOV | DEC |

1 2 3 4 5 6 7 8 9 10 11 12 13 14 15 16 17 18 19 20 21 22 23 24 25 26 27 28 29 30 31

Daily Morning Reset
(For mental clarity + emotional grounding)

Today, my body feels…

☐ Tense
☐ Rested
☐ Scattered
☐ Heavy
☐ Neutral
☐ Something else: _____

One thing weighing on me today is…

_____
_____
_____
_____
_____

Emotion I'm carrying into today:

_____
_____
_____
_____

What I need emotionally right now:

☐ Space
☐ Encouragement
☐ Boundaries
☐ Rest
☐ Focus
☐ Connection
☐ Other: _____

My intention for today:
A sentence or two that feels doable, gentle, and honest.

_____
_____
_____

A micro-practice to begin the day:
(Choose one)

- 1-minute grounding breath

- Soften your jaw + drop your shoulders

- Step outside for 3 deep breaths

- Name three things supporting you today

Daily Evening Reflection Pages
(For emotional processing + nervous system unwinding)

Where did stress show up today?

Body: _____
Mind: _____
Emotions: _____

How did I respond?

☐ Reacted quickly
☐ Shut down
☐ Over-functioned
☐ Avoided
☐ Paused
☐ Responded intentionally

Notes:
_____
_____
_____

What part of me needed more care?
_____
_____
_____
_____

A moment I'm proud of today:
_____
_____
_____
_____
_____

Something I want to release tonight:
_____
_____
_____
_____
_____
_____

Notes:
_____
_____
_____

Closing breath cue:
Inhale for 4, hold for 2, exhale for 6 — repeat 3 times.

Weekly Reflection

Energy Check-In

What drained me this week?

_____
_____
_____

What restored me this week?

_____
_____
_____

Emotional Patterns I Noticed

- When did I override myself?

- When did I honor my capacity?

- What emotion repeated most?

Notes:

_____
_____

A boundary I need for next week:

_____
_____

One small shift that would support me next week:

_____
_____

Weekly Stress Pattern Awareness Worksheet

What My Stress Cycle This Week Looked Like:

Trigger → Reaction → Emotion → Behavior → Aftermath

Trigger: _____　Trigger: _____　Trigger: _____
Reaction: _____　Reaction: _____　Reaction: _____
Emotion: _____　Emotion: _____　Emotion: _____
Behavior: _____　Behavior: _____　Behavior: _____
Aftermath: _____　Aftermath: _____　Aftermath: _____

What my body did under stress:

- ☐ Tight chest
- ☐ Stomach tension
- ☐ Shallow breathing
- ☐ Head pressure
- ☐ Frozen / shut down
- ☐ Other: _____

What I needed in those moments:

- ☐ Slowness
- ☐ Clarity
- ☐ Space
- ☐ Reassurance
- ☐ Regulation
- ☐ Boundaries

Notes:

_____

_____

JAN	FEB	MAR	APR	MAY	JUN	JUL	AUG	SEP	OCT	NOV	DEC

1 2 3 4 5 6 7 8 9 10 11 12 13 14 15 16 17 18 19 20 21 22 23 24 25 26 27 28 29 30 31

Daily Morning Reset
(For mental clarity + emotional grounding)

Today, my body feels…

☐ Tense
☐ Rested
☐ Scattered
☐ Heavy
☐ Neutral
☐ Something else: _____

One thing weighing on me today is…

_____
_____
_____
_____
_____

Emotion I'm carrying into today:

_____
_____
_____
_____

What I need emotionally right now:

☐ Space
☐ Encouragement
☐ Boundaries
☐ Rest
☐ Focus
☐ Connection
☐ Other: _____

My intention for today:
A sentence or two that feels doable, gentle, and honest.

_____
_____
_____

A micro-practice to begin the day:
(Choose one)

- 1-minute grounding breath

- Soften your jaw + drop your shoulders

- Step outside for 3 deep breaths

- Name three things supporting you today

Daily Evening Reflection Pages
(For emotional processing + nervous system unwinding)

Where did stress show up today?

Body: _____
Mind: _____
Emotions: _____

How did I respond?

☐ Reacted quickly
☐ Shut down
☐ Over-functioned
☐ Avoided
☐ Paused
☐ Responded intentionally

Notes:
_____
_____
_____

What part of me needed more care?

_____
_____
_____
_____

A moment I'm proud of today:
_____
_____
_____
_____
_____
_____

Something I want to release tonight:
_____
_____
_____
_____
_____
_____

Notes:
_____
_____
_____

Closing breath cue:

Inhale for 4, hold for 2, exhale for 6 — repeat 3 times.

JAN	FEB	MAR	APR	MAY	JUN	JUL	AUG	SEP	OCT	NOV	DEC

1 2 3 4 5 6 7 8 9 10 11 12 13 14 15 16 17 18 19 20 21 22 23 24 25 26 27 28 29 30 31

Daily Morning Reset
(For mental clarity + emotional grounding)

Today, my body feels...

☐ Tense
☐ Rested
☐ Scattered
☐ Heavy
☐ Neutral
☐ Something else: _____

One thing weighing on me today is...

_____
_____
_____
_____
_____

Emotion I'm carrying into today:

_____
_____
_____
_____
_____

What I need emotionally right now:

☐ Space
☐ Encouragement
☐ Boundaries
☐ Rest
☐ Focus
☐ Connection
☐ Other: _____

My intention for today:

A sentence or two that feels doable, gentle, and honest.

_____
_____
_____

A micro-practice to begin the day:

(Choose one)

- 1-minute grounding breath

- Soften your jaw + drop your shoulders

- Step outside for 3 deep breaths

- Name three things supporting you today

Daily Evening Reflection Pages
(For emotional processing + nervous system unwinding)

Where did stress show up today?

Body: _____
Mind: _____
Emotions: _____

How did I respond?

☐ Reacted quickly
☐ Shut down
☐ Over-functioned
☐ Avoided
☐ Paused
☐ Responded intentionally

Notes:
_____
_____
_____

What part of me needed more care?
_____
_____
_____
_____

A moment I'm proud of today:

_____
_____
_____
_____
_____

Something I want to release tonight:

_____
_____
_____
_____
_____

Notes:

_____
_____
_____

Closing breath cue:

Inhale for 4, hold for 2, exhale for 6 — repeat 3 times.

JAN FEB MAR APR MAY JUN JUL AUG SEP OCT NOV DEC
1 2 3 4 5 6 7 8 9 10 11 12 13 14 15 16 17 18 19 20 21 22 23 24 25 26 27 28 29 30 31

Daily Morning Reset

(For mental clarity + emotional grounding)

Today, my body feels…

☐ Tense
☐ Rested
☐ Scattered
☐ Heavy
☐ Neutral
☐ Something else: _____

One thing weighing on me today is…

_____
_____
_____
_____

Emotion I'm carrying into today:

_____
_____
_____
_____

What I need emotionally right now:

☐ Space
☐ Encouragement
☐ Boundaries
☐ Rest
☐ Focus
☐ Connection
☐ Other: _____

My intention for today:
A sentence or two that feels doable, gentle, and honest.

_____
_____
_____

A micro-practice to begin the day:
(Choose one)

- 1-minute grounding breath

- Soften your jaw + drop your shoulders

- Step outside for 3 deep breaths

- Name three things supporting you today

Daily Evening Reflection Pages
(For emotional processing + nervous system unwinding)

Where did stress show up today?

Body: _____
Mind: _____
Emotions: _____

How did I respond?

☐ Reacted quickly
☐ Shut down
☐ Over-functioned
☐ Avoided
☐ Paused
☐ Responded intentionally

Notes:
_____
_____
_____

What part of me needed more care?

_____
_____
_____
_____

A moment I'm proud of today:
_____
_____
_____
_____
_____

Something I want to release tonight:
_____
_____
_____
_____
_____

Notes:
_____
_____
_____

Closing breath cue:

Inhale for 4, hold for 2, exhale for 6 — repeat 3 times.

| JAN | FEB | MAR | APR | MAY | JUN | JUL | AUG | SEP | OCT | NOV | DEC |

1 2 3 4 5 6 7 8 9 10 11 12 13 14 15 16 17 18 19 20 21 22 23 24 25 26 27 28 29 30 31

Daily Morning Reset

(For mental clarity + emotional grounding)

Today, my body feels…

- ☐ Tense
- ☐ Rested
- ☐ Scattered
- ☐ Heavy
- ☐ Neutral
- ☐ Something else: _____

One thing weighing on me today is…

_____
_____
_____
_____
_____

Emotion I'm carrying into today:

_____
_____
_____
_____
_____

What I need emotionally right now:

☐ Space
☐ Encouragement
☐ Boundaries
☐ Rest
☐ Focus
☐ Connection
☐ Other: _____

My intention for today:

A sentence or two that feels doable, gentle, and honest.

_____
_____
_____

A micro-practice to begin the day:

(Choose one)

- 1-minute grounding breath

- Soften your jaw + drop your shoulders

- Step outside for 3 deep breaths

- Name three things supporting you today

Daily Evening Reflection Pages
(For emotional processing + nervous system unwinding)

Where did stress show up today?

Body: _____
Mind: _____
Emotions: _____

How did I respond?

☐ Reacted quickly
☐ Shut down
☐ Over-functioned
☐ Avoided
☐ Paused
☐ Responded intentionally

Notes:
_____
_____
_____

What part of me needed more care?

_____
_____
_____
_____

A moment I'm proud of today:
_____
_____
_____
_____
_____

Something I want to release tonight:
_____
_____
_____
_____
_____

Notes:
_____
_____
_____

Closing breath cue:

Inhale for 4, hold for 2, exhale for 6 — repeat 3 times.

| JAN | FEB | MAR | APR | MAY | JUN | JUL | AUG | SEP | OCT | NOV | DEC |

1 2 3 4 5 6 7 8 9 10 11 12 13 14 15 16 17 18 19 20 21 22 23 24 25 26 27 28 29 30 31

Daily Morning Reset
(For mental clarity + emotional grounding)

Today, my body feels...

☐ Tense
☐ Rested
☐ Scattered
☐ Heavy
☐ Neutral
☐ Something else: _____

One thing weighing on me today is...

_____
_____
_____
_____
_____

Emotion I'm carrying into today:

_____
_____
_____
_____
_____

What I need emotionally right now:

☐ Space
☐ Encouragement
☐ Boundaries
☐ Rest
☐ Focus
☐ Connection
☐ Other: _____

My intention for today:
A sentence or two that feels doable, gentle, and honest.

_____
_____
_____

A micro-practice to begin the day:
(Choose one)

- 1-minute grounding breath

- Soften your jaw + drop your shoulders

- Step outside for 3 deep breaths

- Name three things supporting you today

Daily Evening Reflection Pages
(For emotional processing + nervous system unwinding)

Where did stress show up today?

Body: _____

Mind: _____

Emotions: _____

How did I respond?

☐ Reacted quickly
☐ Shut down
☐ Over-functioned
☐ Avoided
☐ Paused
☐ Responded intentionally

Notes:
_____
_____
_____

What part of me needed more care?

_____
_____
_____
_____

A moment I'm proud of today:
_____
_____
_____
_____
_____

Something I want to release tonight:
_____
_____
_____
_____
_____

Notes:
_____
_____
_____

Closing breath cue:

Inhale for 4, hold for 2, exhale for 6 — repeat 3 times.

JAN FEB MAR APR MAY JUN JUL AUG SEP OCT NOV DEC
1 2 3 4 5 6 7 8 9 10 11 12 13 14 15 16 17 18 19 20 21 22 23 24 25 26 27 28 29 30 31

Daily Morning Reset
(For mental clarity + emotional grounding)

Today, my body feels…

☐ Tense
☐ Rested
☐ Scattered
☐ Heavy
☐ Neutral
☐ Something else: _____

One thing weighing on me today is…

_____
_____
_____
_____

Emotion I'm carrying into today:

_____
_____
_____
_____
_____

What I need emotionally right now:

☐ Space
☐ Encouragement
☐ Boundaries
☐ Rest
☐ Focus
☐ Connection
☐ Other: _____

My intention for today:
A sentence or two that feels doable, gentle, and honest.

_____
_____
_____

A micro-practice to begin the day:
(Choose one)

- 1-minute grounding breath

- Soften your jaw + drop your shoulders

- Step outside for 3 deep breaths

- Name three things supporting you today

Daily Evening Reflection Pages
(For emotional processing + nervous system unwinding)

Where did stress show up today?

Body: _____
Mind: _____
Emotions: _____

How did I respond?

☐ Reacted quickly
☐ Shut down
☐ Over-functioned
☐ Avoided
☐ Paused
☐ Responded intentionally

Notes:
_____
_____
_____

What part of me needed more care?

_____
_____
_____
_____

A moment I'm proud of today:
_____
_____
_____
_____
_____

Something I want to release tonight:
_____
_____
_____
_____
_____

Notes:
_____
_____
_____

Closing breath cue:

Inhale for 4, hold for 2, exhale for 6 — repeat 3 times.

JAN FEB MAR APR MAY JUN JUL AUG SEP OCT NOV DEC
1 2 3 4 5 6 7 8 9 10 11 12 13 14 15 16 17 18 19 20 21 22 23 24 25 26 27 28 29 30 31

Daily Morning Reset

(For mental clarity + emotional grounding)

Today, my body feels…

☐ Tense
☐ Rested
☐ Scattered
☐ Heavy
☐ Neutral
☐ Something else: _____

One thing weighing on me today is…

_____
_____
_____
_____

Emotion I'm carrying into today:

_____
_____
_____
_____

What I need emotionally right now:

☐ Space
☐ Encouragement
☐ Boundaries
☐ Rest
☐ Focus
☐ Connection
☐ Other: _____

My intention for today:

A sentence or two that feels doable, gentle, and honest.

_____
_____
_____

A micro-practice to begin the day:
(Choose one)

- 1-minute grounding breath

- Soften your jaw + drop your shoulders

- Step outside for 3 deep breaths

- Name three things supporting you today

Daily Evening Reflection Pages

(For emotional processing + nervous system unwinding)

Where did stress show up today?

Body: _____
Mind: _____
Emotions: _____

How did I respond?

☐ Reacted quickly
☐ Shut down
☐ Over-functioned
☐ Avoided
☐ Paused
☐ Responded intentionally

Notes:
_____
_____
_____

What part of me needed more care?
_____
_____
_____

A moment I'm proud of today:

_____
_____
_____
_____
_____
_____

Something I want to release tonight:

_____
_____
_____
_____
_____
_____

Notes:

_____
_____
_____

Closing breath cue:

Inhale for 4, hold for 2, exhale for 6 — repeat 3 times.

Weekly Reflection

Energy Check-In

What drained me this week?

_____
_____
_____

What restored me this week?

_____
_____
_____

Emotional Patterns I Noticed

- When did I override myself?

- When did I honor my capacity?

- What emotion repeated most?

Notes:

_____
_____

A boundary I need for next week:

_____
_____

One small shift that would support me next week:

_____
_____

Weekly Stress Pattern Awareness Worksheet

What My Stress Cycle This Week Looked Like:

Trigger → Reaction → Emotion → Behavior → Aftermath

Trigger: _____	Trigger: _____	Trigger: _____
Reaction: _____	Reaction: _____	Reaction: _____
Emotion: _____	Emotion: _____	Emotion: _____
Behavior: _____	Behavior: _____	Behavior: _____
Aftermath: _____	Aftermath: _____	Aftermath: _____

What my body did under stress:

- ☐ Tight chest
- ☐ Stomach tension
- ☐ Shallow breathing
- ☐ Head pressure
- ☐ Frozen / shut down
- ☐ Other: _____

What I needed in those moments:

- ☐ Slowness
- ☐ Clarity
- ☐ Space
- ☐ Reassurance
- ☐ Regulation
- ☐ Boundaries

Notes:

_____

_____

| JAN | FEB | MAR | APR | MAY | JUN | JUL | AUG | SEP | OCT | NOV | DEC |

1 2 3 4 5 6 7 8 9 10 11 12 13 14 15 16 17 18 19 20 21 22 23 24 25 26 27 28 29 30 31

Daily Morning Reset
(For mental clarity + emotional grounding)

Today, my body feels…

☐ Tense
☐ Rested
☐ Scattered
☐ Heavy
☐ Neutral
☐ Something else: _____

One thing weighing on me today is…

_____
_____
_____
_____
_____

Emotion I'm carrying into today:

_____
_____
_____
_____
_____

What I need emotionally right now:

☐ Space
☐ Encouragement
☐ Boundaries
☐ Rest
☐ Focus
☐ Connection
☐ Other: _____

My intention for today:
A sentence or two that feels doable, gentle, and honest.

_____
_____

A micro-practice to begin the day:
(Choose one)

- 1-minute grounding breath

- Soften your jaw + drop your shoulders

- Step outside for 3 deep breaths

- Name three things supporting you today

Daily Evening Reflection Pages
(For emotional processing + nervous system unwinding)

Where did stress show up today?

Body: _____
Mind: _____
Emotions: _____

How did I respond?

☐ Reacted quickly
☐ Shut down
☐ Over-functioned
☐ Avoided
☐ Paused
☐ Responded intentionally

Notes:
_____
_____
_____

What part of me needed more care?

_____
_____
_____

A moment I'm proud of today:
_____
_____
_____
_____
_____

Something I want to release tonight:
_____
_____
_____
_____
_____
_____

Notes:
_____
_____
_____

Closing breath cue:

Inhale for 4, hold for 2, exhale for 6 — repeat 3 times.

JAN FEB MAR APR MAY JUN JUL AUG SEP OCT NOV DEC
1 2 3 4 5 6 7 8 9 10 11 12 13 14 15 16 17 18 19 20 21 22 23 24 25 26 27 28 29 30 31

Daily Morning Reset

(For mental clarity + emotional grounding)

Today, my body feels...

☐ Tense
☐ Rested
☐ Scattered
☐ Heavy
☐ Neutral
☐ Something else: _____

One thing weighing on me today is...

_____
_____
_____
_____
_____

Emotion I'm carrying into today:

_____
_____
_____
_____
_____

What I need emotionally right now:

☐ Space
☐ Encouragement
☐ Boundaries
☐ Rest
☐ Focus
☐ Connection
☐ Other: _____

My intention for today:
A sentence or two that feels doable, gentle, and honest.

_____
_____
_____

A micro-practice to begin the day:
(Choose one)

- 1-minute grounding breath

- Soften your jaw + drop your shoulders

- Step outside for 3 deep breaths

- Name three things supporting you today

Daily Evening Reflection Pages
(For emotional processing + nervous system unwinding)

Where did stress show up today?

Body: _____
Mind: _____
Emotions: _____

How did I respond?

☐ Reacted quickly
☐ Shut down
☐ Over-functioned
☐ Avoided
☐ Paused
☐ Responded intentionally

Notes:
_____
_____
_____

What part of me needed more care?

_____
_____
_____
_____

A moment I'm proud of today:
_____
_____
_____
_____
_____
_____

Something I want to release tonight:
_____
_____
_____
_____
_____
_____

Notes:
_____
_____
_____

Closing breath cue:

Inhale for 4, hold for 2, exhale for 6 — repeat 3 times.

JAN	FEB	MAR	APR	MAY	JUN	JUL	AUG	SEP	OCT	NOV	DEC

1 2 3 4 5 6 7 8 9 10 11 12 13 14 15 16 17 18 19 20 21 22 23 24 25 26 27 28 29 30 31

Daily Morning Reset
(For mental clarity + emotional grounding)

Today, my body feels…

☐ Tense
☐ Rested
☐ Scattered
☐ Heavy
☐ Neutral
☐ Something else: _____

One thing weighing on me today is…

_____
_____
_____
_____

Emotion I'm carrying into today:

_____
_____
_____
_____

What I need emotionally right now:

☐ Space
☐ Encouragement
☐ Boundaries
☐ Rest
☐ Focus
☐ Connection
☐ Other: _____

My intention for today:
A sentence or two that feels doable, gentle, and honest.

_____
_____
_____

A micro-practice to begin the day:
(Choose one)

- 1-minute grounding breath

- Soften your jaw + drop your shoulders

- Step outside for 3 deep breaths

- Name three things supporting you today

Daily Evening Reflection Pages
(For emotional processing + nervous system unwinding)

Where did stress show up today?

Body: _____
Mind: _____
Emotions: _____

How did I respond?

☐ Reacted quickly
☐ Shut down
☐ Over-functioned
☐ Avoided
☐ Paused
☐ Responded intentionally

Notes:
_____
_____
_____

What part of me needed more care?
_____
_____
_____
_____

A moment I'm proud of today:
_____
_____
_____
_____
_____

Something I want to release tonight:
_____
_____
_____
_____
_____

Notes:
_____
_____
_____

Closing breath cue:

Inhale for 4, hold for 2, exhale for 6 — repeat 3 times.

JAN　　FEB　　MAR　　APR　　MAY　　JUN　　JUL　　AUG　　SEP　　OCT　　NOV　　DEC
1　2　3　4　5　6　7　8　9　10　11　12　13　14　15　16　17　18　19　20　21　22　23　24　25　26　27　28　29　30　31

Daily Morning Reset

(For mental clarity + emotional grounding)

Today, my body feels...

☐ Tense
☐ Rested
☐ Scattered
☐ Heavy
☐ Neutral
☐ Something else: _____

One thing weighing on me today is...

_____
_____
_____
_____
_____

Emotion I'm carrying into today:

_____
_____
_____
_____
_____

What I need emotionally right now:

☐ Space
☐ Encouragement
☐ Boundaries
☐ Rest
☐ Focus
☐ Connection
☐ Other: _____

My intention for today:
A sentence or two that feels doable, gentle, and honest.

_____
_____
_____

A micro-practice to begin the day:
(Choose one)

- 1-minute grounding breath

- Soften your jaw + drop your shoulders

- Step outside for 3 deep breaths

- Name three things supporting you today

Daily Evening Reflection Pages
(For emotional processing + nervous system unwinding)

Where did stress show up today?

Body: _____
Mind: _____
Emotions: _____

How did I respond?

☐ Reacted quickly
☐ Shut down
☐ Over-functioned
☐ Avoided
☐ Paused
☐ Responded intentionally

Notes:
_____
_____
_____

What part of me needed more care?
_____
_____
_____
_____

A moment I'm proud of today:
_____
_____
_____
_____
_____

Something I want to release tonight:
_____
_____
_____
_____
_____

Notes:
_____
_____

Closing breath cue:
Inhale for 4, hold for 2, exhale for 6 — repeat 3 times.

JAN FEB MAR APR MAY JUN JUL AUG SEP OCT NOV DEC
1 2 3 4 5 6 7 8 9 10 11 12 13 14 15 16 17 18 19 20 21 22 23 24 25 26 27 28 29 30 31

Daily Morning Reset

(For mental clarity + emotional grounding)

Today, my body feels...

- ☐ Tense
- ☐ Rested
- ☐ Scattered
- ☐ Heavy
- ☐ Neutral
- ☐ Something else: _____

One thing weighing on me today is...

_____
_____
_____
_____
_____

Emotion I'm carrying into today:

_____
_____
_____
_____

What I need emotionally right now:

☐ Space
☐ Encouragement
☐ Boundaries
☐ Rest
☐ Focus
☐ Connection
☐ Other: _____

My intention for today:
A sentence or two that feels doable, gentle, and honest.

_____
_____
_____

A micro-practice to begin the day:
(Choose one)

- 1-minute grounding breath

- Soften your jaw + drop your shoulders

- Step outside for 3 deep breaths

- Name three things supporting you today

Daily Evening Reflection Pages
(For emotional processing + nervous system unwinding)

Where did stress show up today?

Body: _____
Mind: _____
Emotions: _____

How did I respond?

☐ Reacted quickly
☐ Shut down
☐ Over-functioned
☐ Avoided
☐ Paused
☐ Responded intentionally

Notes:
_____
_____

What part of me needed more care?
_____
_____
_____

A moment I'm proud of today:
_____
_____
_____
_____
_____

Something I want to release tonight:
_____
_____
_____
_____
_____

Notes:
_____
_____
_____

Closing breath cue:

Inhale for 4, hold for 2, exhale for 6 — repeat 3 times.

JAN　FEB　MAR　APR　MAY　JUN　JUL　AUG　SEP　OCT　NOV　DEC
1　2　3　4　5　6　7　8　9　10　11　12　13　14　15　16　17　18　19　20　21　22　23　24　25　26　27　28　29　30　31

Daily Morning Reset
(For mental clarity + emotional grounding)

Today, my body feels...

- ☐ Tense
- ☐ Rested
- ☐ Scattered
- ☐ Heavy
- ☐ Neutral
- ☐ Something else: _____

One thing weighing on me today is...

_____
_____
_____
_____
_____

Emotion I'm carrying into today:

_____
_____
_____
_____
_____

What I need emotionally right now:

☐ Space
☐ Encouragement
☐ Boundaries
☐ Rest
☐ Focus
☐ Connection
☐ Other: _____

My intention for today:
A sentence or two that feels doable, gentle, and honest.

_____
_____
_____

A micro-practice to begin the day:
(Choose one)

- 1-minute grounding breath

- Soften your jaw + drop your shoulders

- Step outside for 3 deep breaths

- Name three things supporting you today

Daily Evening Reflection Pages
(For emotional processing + nervous system unwinding)

Where did stress show up today?

Body: _____
Mind: _____
Emotions: _____

How did I respond?

- ☐ Reacted quickly
- ☐ Shut down
- ☐ Over-functioned
- ☐ Avoided
- ☐ Paused
- ☐ Responded intentionally

Notes:
_____
_____
_____

What part of me needed more care?

_____
_____
_____

A moment I'm proud of today:
_____
_____
_____
_____
_____

Something I want to release tonight:
_____
_____
_____
_____
_____

Notes:
_____
_____
_____

Closing breath cue:

Inhale for 4, hold for 2, exhale for 6 — repeat 3 times.

| JAN | FEB | MAR | APR | MAY | JUN | JUL | AUG | SEP | OCT | NOV | DEC |

1 2 3 4 5 6 7 8 9 10 11 12 13 14 15 16 17 18 19 20 21 22 23 24 25 26 27 28 29 30 31

Daily Morning Reset
(For mental clarity + emotional grounding)

Today, my body feels...

☐ Tense
☐ Rested
☐ Scattered
☐ Heavy
☐ Neutral
☐ Something else: _____

One thing weighing on me today is...

_____
_____
_____
_____
_____

Emotion I'm carrying into today:

_____
_____
_____
_____
_____

What I need emotionally right now:

☐ Space
☐ Encouragement
☐ Boundaries
☐ Rest
☐ Focus
☐ Connection
☐ Other: _____

My intention for today:
A sentence or two that feels doable, gentle, and honest.

_____
_____
_____

A micro-practice to begin the day:
(Choose one)

- 1-minute grounding breath

- Soften your jaw + drop your shoulders

- Step outside for 3 deep breaths

- Name three things supporting you today

Daily Evening Reflection Pages
(For emotional processing + nervous system unwinding)

Where did stress show up today?

Body: _____
Mind: _____
Emotions: _____

How did I respond?

☐ Reacted quickly
☐ Shut down
☐ Over-functioned
☐ Avoided
☐ Paused
☐ Responded intentionally

Notes:
_____
_____
_____

What part of me needed more care?
_____
_____
_____
_____

A moment I'm proud of today:

_____
_____
_____
_____
_____

Something I want to release tonight:

_____
_____
_____
_____
_____

Notes:

_____
_____

Closing breath cue:
Inhale for 4, hold for 2, exhale for 6 — repeat 3 times.

Weekly Reflection

Energy Check-In

What drained me this week?

_____
_____
_____

What restored me this week?

_____
_____
_____

Emotional Patterns I Noticed

- When did I override myself?

- When did I honor my capacity?

- What emotion repeated most?

Notes:
_____
_____

A boundary I need for next week:

_____
_____

One small shift that would support me next week:

_____
_____

Weekly Stress Pattern Awareness Worksheet

What My Stress Cycle This Week Looked Like:

Trigger → Reaction → Emotion → Behavior → Aftermath

Trigger: _____ Trigger: _____ Trigger: _____
Reaction: _____ Reaction: _____ Reaction: _____
Emotion: _____ Emotion: _____ Emotion: _____
Behavior: _____ Behavior: _____ Behavior: _____
Aftermath: _____ Aftermath: _____ Aftermath: _____

What my body did under stress:

- ☐ Tight chest
- ☐ Stomach tension
- ☐ Shallow breathing
- ☐ Head pressure
- ☐ Frozen / shut down
- ☐ Other: _____

What I needed in those moments:

- ☐ Slowness
- ☐ Clarity
- ☐ Space
- ☐ Reassurance
- ☐ Regulation
- ☐ Boundaries

Notes:
_____
_____

www.ingramcontent.com/pod-product-compliance
Lightning Source LLC
Chambersburg PA
CBHW070742060526
44119CB00071B/119